Royal SANDRINGHAM

Royal SANDRINGHAM

**Albert Edward
Prince of Wales
1863-1901**

**King Edward VII
1901-1910**

**Queen Alexandra
1910-1925**

**King George V
1925-1936**

**King Edward VIII
1936**

**King George VI
1936-1952**

**Queen Elizabeth II
1952-**

by Philip Hepworth

Edited and designed by
Michael Shaw

 Wensum

WENSUM BOOKS (NORWICH) LTD
33 Orford Place
Norwich NR1 3QA

First published July 1978
ISBN 0 903619 25 3

Printed by Euromedia Print Ltd, Norwich
Bound by Webb Son & Co Ltd, London

Contents

Foreword

This history of the Royal estates at Sandringham in Norfolk is one in which the illustrations are at least as important as the text. During Queen Victoria's reign (1837-1901) when Sandringham was acquired by the Royal Family, the art of photography developed from stilted beginnings until it surpassed painting, drawing, and engraving as the normal method of recording life's formal and informal occasions. The Royal Family had welcomed and participated in the new art ever since Albert the Prince Consort sat for his first photograph in 1842.[1] His eldest son's acquisition of Sandringham Hall in 1862 coincided with the initial general availability of F. S. Archer's wet collodion process, invented in 1851. Glass negatives had come into use a few years earlier and these two changes marked a great improvement in definition over the previous calotype process, using paper negatives, invented by Fox Talbot in 1841.

So photographs predominate in our work, many of them taken in the nineteenth century and, with few exceptions, all on the Sandringham estate.

My chief indebtedness is to Her Majesty the Queen, who has graciously permitted the use of certain material relating to the estate, including photographs, from the Royal Archives. I should also like to express my gratitude to those members of the Royal Household who have given further information and guidance.

To Desmond Buxton, D.L., of Hoveton Hall, I am very grateful for permission to use his grandmother's delightful account of a ball at Sandringham in 1873.

Philip Hepworth
Norwich 1978

THE PRESENT ROYAL ESTATE of Sandringham lies some eight miles north-east of King's Lynn. Two escarpments rise up at the edge of the Fens and Sandringham lies between them in a sandy area of heaths and woodlands, with outcrops of a red rock known locally as 'carstone'. Because of the poor soil the area has traditionally been given over to shooting. The easily burrowed soil abounded with rabbits, whose skins formed a substantial fur and felt trade centred on Brandon. In the last two centuries the introduction of coniferous trees has proved successful and today they lend a distinctive character to the area.

The village of Sandringham is mentioned in the 'Domesday Book' (1086) as 'Sant Dersingham'[1] – the sandy part of Dersingham, the village one mile to the north. There is evidence of a residence there as early as 1296. From the early sixteenth century the district was dominated by two families. The Roman Catholic Cobbes held the land from 1517 to 1686 when they were succeeded by the Protestant Hostes. The successive heads of these families held to their estates through all adversity against a backcloth of political and religious upheaval. In 1752 the Hoste fortunes descended to a woman, Susan Hoste, who was successfully courted by Cornish Henley of Leigh House in Somerset. At the time of their marriage the couple were both twenty-two years old.

Coupling his wife's surname with his own, Cornish Hoste Henley elected to live at Sandringham. Mrs Herbert Jones, who before her marriage lived with her father, the patriarchal Daniel Hay Gurney, at near-by North Runcton Hall, recalled Sandringham House as being spoken of as 'a long low house with wings, and rather small windows; the staircase, forgotten in the alterations, awkwardly penetrating the roof of the Hall'.[2]

1 Early History
1752-1862

The entry relating to Sandringham in the 'Domesday Book' (1086). Translated it reads: Santdersinham (Sandringham) is held by Ranulf, which one freeman held under Harold in the time of King Edward the Confessor . . . 1 plough; now none. 5 bordars; now none. 3 serfs; now 1 and 3½ acres of meadow. Then and later 1 plough belonging to the men . . . 1 saltpan then as now worth 20 shillings.

R. H. Mason *c.* 1865

Norfolk County Libraries

An early picture of the west front of
Sandringham Hall built by Cornish Hoste
Henley in 1771.

Cornish Hoste Henley all but demolished the old house[3] (possibly Elizabethan) and erected in its place a three-storey house built back to back and constituting as Mrs Herbert Jones said 'almost a new edifice'.[4] The old house had apparently been built round three sides of a square. The new was 'an ungainly house, a robust slate-roofed block or rather a huddle of blocks, as if a giant had rammed two oblong boxes of uneven length side by side, and then roofed them separately filling out the nooks and corners of these parallel but unequal ranges with four prim cubes, each with a separate roof and chimney'.[5]

The main alterations were completed by about 1771, the year in which the agriculturist Arthur Young described the estate: 'About Sandringham, the seat of Henry Cornish Henley, Esq. are very considerable tracts of sandy land, which are applied only at present to feeding of rabbits; it is a very barren soil but not I apprehend incapable of cultivation; it lets from 1s 6d to 2s 6d an acre in warrens; Mr Henley has tried some experiments on it lately, with a view to discovering how far it will answer cultivating. The value of it is prodigiously advanced by planting; that gentleman has formed several plantations, which thrive extremely; all the firs do well; and will pay a better rent for the land than will husbandry.'[6]

In 1773 Cornish Hoste Henley died at the age of forty-one and the estate passed to his seven-year-old son, Henry Hoste Henley. The younger Henley made little alteration to the house or the estate although he refronted Babingley manor-house with carstone in 1820.

Volume 2 of *Excursions in the County of Norfolk* published in 1819 gives only eleven words to 'Sanderingham Hall and park' and the hundred engravings in the work do not include an illustration of it. *Neale's seats* (published in six volumes in 1822-23), perhaps the finest general illustrated topical work of its kind of the period, does not include Sandringham among the twenty-two Norfolk properties described. Bryant's large-scale map of Norfolk of 1826 clearly shows Sandringham as one of the smaller Norfolk properties, remote and less well placed in relation to good roads than many other near-by country-houses; the turnpike road adjoins the estate but is a fair distance from the house.

Henry Hoste Henley had four children all of whom predeceased him. Thus upon his death in 1833 at the age of sixty-seven he was without heir and the estate ultimately came up for auction in 1836.

Sandringham Hall was purchased by a local landowner, John Motteux of Beachamwell Hall, which lay fifteen miles to the south-east. Motteux, a wealthy bachelor of Huguenot descent, had inherited Beachamwell some forty years earlier and was popular both in the village and with the local gentry. He may well have purchased Sandringham for his younger brother Robert, of Banstead Place, Surrey. If so the plan was nullified by the death of Robert, who died before he could be even informed of the purchase.

On the other hand it could have been simply the land which interested him, for throughout his ownership Sandringham remained unoccupied and unfurnished. He made no attempt to stop the auction of the house's contents by Henry Hoste Henley's executors. These included a Bible and a portrait of a relative of the Hostes who had been burned at the stake, but there is little reason to think that the Henleys had acquired more than conventional books and furnishings of the time or that the stuffed animals which were sold off were any great loss. In fact the value of the furniture, plate, books, and brewing materials which had been assessed at £1,567 on Henry Hoste Henley's death, after costs, only realized £635 at auction.[7]

Motteux was a very keen sportsman. When he arranged shoots at Beachamwell, 'he would order the school, which he had himself built and endowed, to be emptied, and the children to be distributed about, to brush the coverts like so many spaniels',[8] but his chief passion was gardening. At Beachamwell he had gained the Royal Horticultural Society's Silver Medal for fruit, and at a London dinner-party where Talleyrand, French

Norfolk Record Office

The Sale Catalogue for Sandringham Hall, issued by the executors of Henry Hoste Henley in 1836.

William Faden 1797   Norfolk Record Society

The first quarter of the nineteenth century was the last great age of individualized Norfolk map-making before the uniformities of the Ordnance Survey. Faden's map of 1797 and Bryant's of 1826 were the outstanding productions of this period. Faden's map even named landowners and here we see H. H. Henley listed against Sandringham.

F. Ralph 1863

Norfolk County Libraries

Ambassador to the Court of St James's (1830-34), was present, he had interested the elder statesman by discoursing on the cultivation of pears. The acreage of Sandringham was increased from 5,400 to 7,000 and some of his boundary-marks, inscribed I.M. (Iohannes Motteux) still remain. He improved both estates with great enthusiasm, planting a great many picturesque trees and shrubberies and it is he who laid the foundation for the fine gardens of today.

When in 1837 he reached the age of seventy, John Motteux, still a bachelor, considered his succession. His oldest friend, the fifth Earl Cowper who had afforded him an introduction into high society, had died

Sandringham Hall from the park. The oldest tree on the estate is an oak dating back to Norman times. Extensive planting, however, was undertaken by both the Henleys and John Motteux.

Norfolk County Libraries

The west front of Sandringham Hall showing
Teulon's conservatory of carstone and brick.

that same year leaving his vivacious widow Emmy with two unmarried
sons on her hands. Two years later when Emmy married Lord Palmerston
the British Foreign Minister, Motteux appreciated that a legacy to one of
her unmarried younger sons would be the most suitable recognition of
their long friendship. Initially the will designated as heir to the estate her
second son, William Francis, but upon his marrying a Gurney scarcely a
month before Motteux's death in 1843, it was changed and her third and
only unmarried son, Charles Spencer Cowper inherited.[9]

Charles was a diplomat, attached to the Swedish Court, and so much in
fear of legal proceedings, possibly for debt, that any missive which
reached him of a legal nature he left unopened. So a full fortnight passed
before he realized he had inherited Sandringham. Charles, busy with his
career and most often abroad, spent little time at Sandringham.[10] In 1852
he married Lady Harriet d'Orsay the widow of the celebrated beau, Count
Alfred d'Orsay (1801-52). A year or two later he engaged the then
fashionable exponent of High Victorian Gothic architecture, Samuel
Sanders Teulon (1812-73) to design balustrades for the garden, and for the
house tall Tudor-style chimneys to cure the smoky fires, a multicoloured
extravagantly decorated entrance porch, and a conservatory.

R. H. Mason *c.* 1865

The east front of Sandringham Hall in the early 1860s, showing Teulon's porch.

His mother, Emmy, whose husband was now Prime Minister, writing on 28 October 1856 said: 'The improvements you mention must be very great and give quite a new appearance to the House, and I am very glad that it should have been done. Everybody likes to improve and to alter. It gives a feeling of ownership, and an interest in your own possession. I think I could easily myself get very fond of Sandringham if I lived there. It is such a nice wild Country with all its sandy drives and extent of heath and gorse and firs.'[11]

The Cowpers owned Sandringham for another six years before it was purchased for the Prince of Wales. Lady Harriet Cowper spent some time there and formed an attachment for the estate and the tenantry. After the sale in 1862, Mrs Herbert Jones reports her as saying, prior to leaving: ' "The large sum of money obtained and the high station of the purchaser were great inducements as we have every reason to hope that the circumstances of the tenantry will be much improved, but I shall regret the Orphan Home, the church, the schools and the kind, good, grateful people." '[12]

13

Caldesi

Radio Times Hulton Picture Library

Queen Victoria and Prince Albert at Osborne
House, Isle of Wight, with their nine children in
1857. The Prince of Wales is on the extreme
right, aged sixteen.

2
Royal
Search
1861-1862

IN 1861 PRINCE ALBERT OF SAXE-COBURG, Prince Consort of Great Britain and
husband of Queen Victoria (1837-1901), was looking for a country-house
for his eldest son, Albert Edward, Prince of Wales, now approaching
twenty. The Prince of Wales traditionally enjoys the revenues of the Duchy
of Cornwall, and during his minority the Prince Consort had supervised the
Cornish estates with such prudence that the annual revenue rose from
£16,000 in 1841 to nearly £60,000 in 1859.

The Prince of Wales had a home of his own, Marlborough House, ap-
propriated to him from the Dowager Queen Adelaide's estate in 1850
although it was still used for governmental purposes for some years more.
Nevertheless the Prince Consort began to put out feelers for a home for
his son lying farther from the centre of administration. Among the properties considered were Newstead Abbey in Nottinghamshire; Hatherop in the
Cotswolds; Somerleyton in Suffolk – 'in a flat park not picturesque. House
magnificent and very costly in construction'; a Scottish property near Loch
Luichart; Chilham Castle in Kent; Moor Park, two miles from Hereford;
and Lynford Hall near Euston in Norfolk.[1]

The Prince of Wales was unquestionably disappointed at not acquiring Newstead. Writing to his father on 5 March 1861 he thought it was too bad that it should have been sold behind the back of Edward White, the Crown Solicitor. Writing later to her husband's biographer Theodore Martin, Queen Victoria expressed her pleasure in her son's avoidance of an association with the wicked Lord Byron by the purchasing of his old home. [2]

The Prince of Wales for his part was reluctant to go to Scotland, even to please his mother. An important factor governing the choice of a country retreat for the Prince seems to have been that it should be far enough away from London for him to escape from the distractions of society and enjoy the benefits of a healthy country life. The house itself should be sited to provide the completest measure of privacy, without being too remote or inaccessible.

That attention ultimately fell upon Sandringham was probably due to other considerations. Sandringham's owner, Charles Spencer Cowper, was the stepson of the Prime Minister, Lord Palmerston. The fact that Cowper might be persuaded to sell could easily have been conveyed to the Prince Consort. Sandringham was certainly isolated and was well screened by trees. Furthermore there were several respected families living in Norfolk who would provide ideal social and sporting companionship for the Prince. The railway line from London to King's Lynn completed in 1847 made the estate easy of access.

It was thought that the rent roll aimed at should be £10,000 per annum. Edward White, the Crown Solicitor, estimated the rent roll at Sandringham to be £7,000, some £3,000 short of what had been hoped for. After some difficulty an option on it was secured from Spencer Cowper but before negotiations were concluded the Prince Consort unexpectedly died of typhoid fever at the early age of forty-two on 14 December 1861. At this terrible blow suffered by his mother, the young Prince of Wales wished only to follow out his father's wishes, especially as just one day after the funeral the Queen had written: 'No human power will make me swerve from what he decided and wished.' [3] Strangely enough, the Prince Consort had himself not visited any of the properties to which he had given so much consideration.

On 3 February 1862, almost two months after his father's death the Prince came up from London by train with members of his Household to visit Sandringham for the first time. At King's Lynn, where the railway then terminated, the party was joined for lunch and for the visit by Edmund Beck, the Sandringham Agent, Spencer Cowper's solicitor, and a Cambridge friend of the Prince, Alfred Thomas Bagge, a future baronet

Engraved by Joseph Brown

When searching for a country home for his eldest son in 1861, the Prince Consort investigated over a score of properties. It could well have been the Prime Minister, Lord Palmerston (1784-1865) who told him of the availability of Sandringham Hall; it belonged to his stepson, Charles Spencer Cowper.

F. Ralph 1863   Norfolk County Libraries

The drive leading to Teulon's porch. This was how the Prince of Wales first viewed the Hall in 1862.

and owner of near-by Stradsett Hall. It was Bagge who pointed out the sights as they passed through the attractive village of Castle Rising and drove through the somewhat unkempt pine and heather approach. Finally the party set eyes on the Hall itself, with Teulon's elaborate red and white porch and, on the garden front, a gable-ended conservatory patterned in red brick and rich brown carstone taken from the near-by quarry at Snettisham, contrasting with the undistinguished white stucco still remaining from the Henleys' mansion. Carstone and flint are practically the only Norfolk building materials. The former is found solely in the west of the county. Used judiciously in thin slabs the gingerbread-coloured stone is most attractive. The Prince of Wales was familiar with the work of the architect Teulon, whose style has since acquired a reputation for extreme ugliness,[4] from the enthusiastic praise of a close friend from his Cambridge University days, the tenth Duke of St Albans.

The Prince tired all his companions by striding round the more adjacent parts of the estate, casting his eye over cattle, pigs, and poultry; finally taking a carriage the distance of the six parishes associated with the proposed purchase. In the afternoon he journeyed back to London with his mind made up – Sandringham was to be his.

For his fore-ordained country-house with its furnishings the Prince paid £220,000, a sum to which his frugal father might not have risen though he had probably some idea of the asking price before his death. The Crown Solicitor had valued Sandringham at £219,000 although John Motteux some twenty-six years earlier had paid only £76,000. The particulars of sale then spoke of 'a mansion replete with every accommodation for a Family of the first respectability, standing on a beautiful lawn and surrounded by a Deer Park and Pleasure Grounds, varied with ornamental Oak, and other thriving Timber and Plantations.' In 1836 the whole estate comprised 5,450 acres, including 'Sandringham, Babingley, and Woolferton [sic]' and was 'one of the finest sporting districts, regularly hunted by the Norfolk Fox Hounds and Harriers, and abounding with Game of every description. . . . The Park, which contains 179 acres . . . is enclosed by a Stone Wall and Park Paling and commands interesting views of the adjacent Country, whilst its declivity and inequality of service . . . add greatly to the beautiful and picturesque appearance. . . . The neighbourhood is excellent, Hillington Hall, the seat of Sir William Folkes, Bart. being within three miles; Houghton Hall, the seat of the Marquis of Cholmondeley within six miles; Lord Townsend's [sic] seat at Rainham, within twelve miles, and Holkham Hall, the seat of T. W. Coke Esq. within sixteen miles. It is also within ten miles of the pleasantly situated Village of Hunstanton, which has a fine sandy Beach, commanding an uninterrupted view of the German Ocean, with other Scenery of a picturesque and beautiful description, and in which are a few private Lodging Houses and Bathing Machines. There is a quarry of carstone on the estate, particularly adapted to building purposes. . . . The Mansion has a Portico entrance. Contiguous is an ornamental Sheet of Water [and] a Grotto, of curious design, lined with Shells, and containing many rare Fossils.' Compared with these delights the summer-house, venison-house, coach-house, straw-house and stable, kennel for hounds, boiling-house and flesh-house were clearly subsidiary.

The date for completion of the purchase was 11 October 1862,[5] but the property was paid for before the end of August.[6]

del. G. F. Sargent 1862   Illustrated London News

The west front of Sandringham Hall described as 'the hunting box of His Royal Highness the Prince of Wales' showing Teulon's conservatory and the proximity of the lake to the house.

THE PRINCE OF WALES was reluctant to accept that Sandringham Hall, un-embellished, was not grand enough for the country home of a future king. On 1 September 1862 he journeyed to Sandringham with a list of recommendations from the Land Steward at Osborne on the Isle of Wight, which his parents had begun to transform into a Royal estate some fifteen years previously. Initially the Prince of Wales thought that the Hall might be made adequate by knocking two reception-rooms into one, but more ambitious plans soon carried him away as his purchase, which included the old manor-house of West Hall, and Wood Hall, had twenty-seven rooms only, apart from the servants' accommodation and cloakrooms.[1]

Apart from the main house, the Prince took an interest in the other properties on his estate. Mrs Louisa Cresswell, a somewhat troublesome tenant of the Prince, complained about her residence, Appleton House. 'Orders were speedily given for the entire demolition of everything as it stood, and the erection of a house and model buildings corresponding as nearly as possible with the plans we [her husband Gerard and herself] had drawn up. Before the pulling down began we were honoured with a visit from our young Royal landlord, then on the eve of his marriage. . . . His Royal Highness was vastly amused with our queer quarters and after looking all round, raced up the ladder of a staircase to see the rooms we had fitted up above, and I need not say how attracted we were with his extraordinary charm of manner and power of putting everyone at their ease, whether they might be driving a donkey cart or cleaning a grate, without a suggestion of patronage or difference of rank. . . . We moved into the new house as soon as the building was sufficiently advanced.'[2]

In the eyes of the Prince Consort it had been as essential for his eldest son to marry as it had been for him to acquire a country-house. The claim of a number of Princesses from all over Europe was considered before a fitting consort was chosen. After a lengthy period of mourning for the death of his father on 10 March 1863 Prince Albert Edward married Princess Alexandra of Denmark. Hailed by Tennyson as 'The sea-king's daughter as happy as fair', she received a more local tribute dedicated by its anonymous author to the Mayor of Lynn:

3
Building the new House
1863-1870

All folks in loyal Lynn declar'd
They'd honour do in fitting way
And that no cost should then be spar'd
To celebrate this great event . . .
The open'd list at bankers lie
And many fives attend the names;
To Stanley* and his mate they cry
For help to speed them in their games
The man of wealth responds most free . . .
The children to their schools now led,
Are soon supplied with beef and bread
And with plum pudding too are fed.
The aged too they now regale
With hearty cheer and good strong ale . . .

* A reference to Lord Stanley, later the fifteenth Earl Derby (1826-93), M.P. for King's Lynn 1848-49, and a notable benefactor to the town.

J. E. Mayall

Radio Times Hulton Picture Library

The Prince and Princess of Wales on their wedding day, 10 May 1863. Queen Victoria still in deep mourning, is gazing upon the bust of her late husband, Prince Albert.

The Sinclair Single-Driver No. 284 decorated
cream with red roses which pulled the train
taking the Prince and Princess of Wales to
Wolferton eighteen days after their wedding.

Great Eastern Railway Magazine

The Prince took his bride to Sandringham for the first time on 28 March
1863, eighteen days after their wedding. The locomotive pulling the Royal
train was painted cream and decorated with red roses. General William
Knollys (1797-1883), the Prince's newly appointed Comptroller, had made
all ready. There was a good stock of venison, vegetables, and claret,
thanks to the housekeeper, Mrs Rugge, 'certainly a valuable utensil',
according to General Knollys.[3] Twenty-four blankets were scarcely
adequate for the present advance party and a further fifty would be
required to complete the bed-linen for thirty-three beds. 'We are rather
cold as all country houses are,' the Comptroller consolingly concluded.[4]

The Prince's instincts made it fairly easy for him to enjoy Sandringham
during the shooting season – his main pursuit there – though at other
times of the year a great deal of his time was perforce spent elsewhere.
Even so he spent Christmas, January, February, his own birthday
(9 November) and Princess Alexandra's (1 December) at Sandringham. The
Prince gave personal attention to the allocation of the bedrooms and
table-places of his guests. On Sundays the Princess and the ladies attended
the full service at the Church of St Mary Magdalene in Sandringham Park,
but the Prince customarily arrived to a fresh peal of bells immediately
before the sermon, which was strictly limited to ten minutes. After
luncheon all guests were conducted by the Prince and Princess on a
lengthy tour of the estate.

The Prince of Wales continued to make extensive alterations to his
estate. New roads were made, cottages were destroyed, lodges built, and re-
landscaping carried out. Fortunately there was an ample supply of men for
all these works from the labour gangs who had been recently working on
the Lynn and Hunstanton Railway.

The Prince and Princess of Wales in the garden of Sandringham Hall during the autumn of 1863.

F. Ralph   Norfolk County Libraries

The Norwich Gates. The motif of the Norwich Gates is a design of arum, oak leaves and acorns, vine leaves and convolvulus, representing the grounds of a country-house. Each one of the four pillars is crowned by a griffin supporting a coloured shield of arms representing the Prince of Wales's various titles. Over all rise the Royal Arms surmounted by a crown, with inlaid sprays of holly and clusters of roses.

A new garden wall had to be built to accommodate the munificent gift of the famous Norwich Gates. These are twenty-five feet high and forty feet wide. A specimen of the ironwork of Thomas Jekyll, they had been constructed by Barnards of Norwich and shown at the 1862 International Exhibition. Jekyll was also the designer of the Pagoda in Chapel Field Gardens, Norwich, which was pulled down some thirty-five years ago. He built run-of-the-mill houses as well as ironwork for Barnards, and established a reputation for supplying wrought-iron gates for owners of private estates. He also designed the Victorian Thorpe St Andrew's Church and restored St Andrew's Church in the Norwich hamlet of Eaton. He had the curious habit of wearing knee-breeches and buckle shoes long after they had ceased to be fashionable. Jekyll went mad in 1877 and died in 1881 without recovering his sanity.

The gates were a wedding-present from the County of Norfolk and the City of Norwich and were presented on 7 April 1863. The ceremony was

The Prince and Princess of Wales in a carriage at the front door of Sandringham Hall in the autumn of 1863.

attended by the High Sheriff (J. S. Scott Chad of Thursford Hall), the Lord-Lieutenant (the Earl of Leicester), the Mayor of Norwich (H.S. Patteson), the Sheriff of Norwich (J. J. Colman), the Mayor of Great Yarmouth (R. Steward), the Mayor of Lynn (L. W. Jarvis, a solicitor who became so friendly with the Prince that he eventually earned the title of Sir Lewis Jarvis), and the Mayor of Thetford (S. C. Bidwell).[5]

Taking up a theme from the High Sheriff's speech, the Prince replied: 'Connected intimately as I now am with Norfolk, I regard with pride so beautiful a specimen of Norwich workmanship and art; and this feeling adds to the pleasure which I could not fail to experience in accepting any offer made by a large body of persons belonging to every class but animated by a common feeling of affectionate goodwill towards myself and the Princess.'[6]

The first full house-party in the old Hall took place in October 1863, the London train depositing its contingent at the newly opened Wolferton Station, two miles distant.*

In that year the Prince made two outings with the West Norfolk Foxhounds, although the fox was only killed on one occasion. In 1865 one of the most brilliant meets in the history of the Hunt took place at Sandringham, the Princess of Wales driving in a phaeton. Years later, Henry Chaplin, the Prince's hunting friend said: 'I always thought hunting was the sport in which the King excelled, far more than in shooting, or in anything else, and I have no doubt that if he had lived in a hunting, instead of a shooting country he would have continued to do so.'

In the early 1860s the Prince embarked on a series of improvements, employing the services of the architect Albert Jenkins Humbert (1822-77). Humbert had worked for the Prince's father enlarging Whippingham Parish Church which adjoined the Queen's home at Osborne on the Isle of Wight. When the Duchess of Kent, Queen Victoria's mother, was in her seventies the Prince Consort asked his Artistic Adviser, Professor Ludwig Gruner, to design a mausoleum for her at Frogmore, near Windsor, and Humbert was appointed to carry out Gruner's designs. The mausoleum was almost complete when the Duchess died. When the Prince Consort's death followed in the same year of 1861 it was natural that Gruner and Humbert should be granted the commission for the Royal Mausoleum to be erected near-by. Speed was their forte; plans were drawn up within a month and in less than a year the mausoleum was ready.

At Sandringham a range of cottages and individual villas were built as well as coach-houses for fifteen vehicles. A villa, Park House, was built for the Prince's Comptroller, General Sir William Knollys. The materials used in its construction consisted of shell carstone (the strongest type), magnesium lime, and artificial stone. The vicarage was completely modernized, and the Lynn double lodges and the Head Gardener's house built. A kitchen, footmen's rooms, a servants' hall, a laundry-room and pump-room with tank appeared, and up the hill in the grounds a private gasworks. For guests down for the shooting Humbert built the so-called Bachelors' Cottage beyond the lake.

The Author 1976

Park House, the residence of the Prince's Comptroller, Sir William Knollys.

Illustrated London News

The Bachelors' Cottage built by Humbert in the mid 1860s for guests of the Prince of Wales.

* R. S. Joby's *Forgotten Railways: East Anglia* (1977) records the date of the opening of the Lynn and Hunstanton Railway as 3 October 1862.

Architecturally these works of Humbert which still stand are admired by purists more than the 'Big House', as the Royal Family termed Humbert's subsequent 1870 construction. Other buildings put up by the Prince at about this time – 1868 – were a model farm, a stud, and a distinctive tall game-store in white brick, with adjoining ice-house. Humbert also converted Teulon's conservatory into a billiard-room for the Prince.

Following on Harriet Spencer Cowper's example, the Princess of Wales set up a school at Sandringham which later developed into the famous Needlework School (for girls) and the Carving School (for boys), Humbert obligingly Gothicizing an old barn which he embellished with ironstone and white brick, standing next to the modernized vicarage.

The Prince was realizing that more and more work would have to be done. In the Library of the Royal Institute of British Architects are some of Humbert's abortive plans for Sandringham including one of a new wing at right angles to the old house, linked by Teulon's conservatory installed by Charles Spencer Cowper and another of the old house with its structure almost completely covered. The Prince refused to accept any of these designs and as late as the Christmas of 1866 the old house was still in use and was, indeed, the scene of social gatherings.

Practically all the Prince of Wales's correspondence was destroyed by his wish after his death as King Edward VII in 1910, so that the reasons why he eventually abandoned improving the country home he had owned for less than five years in favour of a complete rebuilding can only be surmised. The Humbert material at the Royal Institute of British Architects presents so many different schemes for Sandringham (though not the one finally accepted) that it may well have been the architect who intimated in his courteous way that alteration, however extensive, could no longer solve the problem – demolition and replacement being the only answer.

The Prince of Wales may have been influenced by his wife's long illness, commencing in February 1867, though suggestions that the cold and damp had affected her health were muted. Apart from General Knollys' remark on the coldness of all country houses the only extant comment on the cold prevailing at Sandringham Hall was made in 1863 by Lady Macclesfield, the Princess's Lady of the Bedchamber. 'The wind blows keen from the Wash and the Spring is said to be unendurable in that part of Norfolk.'[7] Sir James Paget, the Surgeon in attendance on the Princess stated that rheumatism could be caused by dampness and that Sandringham Hall might well be damp.[8]

On 15 November 1867 the Prince was still writing nostalgically and affectionately to his mother about improvements to the existing house rather than of plans for a new one: 'it is lovely weather and almost too mild.

B. Lemere 1889   Reproduced by gracious permission of Her Majesty the Queen

The billiard-room which was built within Teulon's conservatory by Humbert.

1871   The Graphic

Following Harriet Spencer Cowper's example in 1858, the Royal occupants of Sandringham provided for the education of both girls and boys connected with their estate workers. Originally there was one school, converted from a barn by A. R. Humbert, with Gothic embellishments; it is here shown in 1871 being visited by the Princess of Wales and Prince Albert Victor. The boys later moved into a building on the eastern side, now part of the Museum, the girls continuing in the original building, which is now the Sandringham organist's house. The boys used only hand tools; some of their cabinet-work was of a very high quality and found its way to Potsdam for Kaiser Wilhelm II, and to the Winter Palace in St. Petersburg for Tsar Nicholas II. The Ideal Home Exhibition regularly showed the Schools' work.

I have been very busy all day going about and seeing after the different works. . . . A great part of the new offices are now inhabited. . . . It is a matter of great importance that servants should be properly lodged and to make them as comfortable as possible without spoiling them. I am glad you are not coming here till next year as everywhere is looking so untidy. . . . Mr Onslow [the rector] dined with us.' The Prince then speaks of 'my *own* farm – which is now completed. I shall exhibit the beasts at the Smithfield Cattle Show but hardly expect to get any prize yet. My cold is much better. I have gas everywhere (of course not in the living rooms).'[9] The Queen's letter in reply, dated 22November, assumes that the Prince is going too far too fast; 'We took from [18]45 to [18]61 to make Osborne.'[10] Christmas 1867 was spent at Park House, the Comptroller's residence, the old, Hall, standing gloomily unoccupied.

Probably before 1868 dawned Humbert had received the definite order to demolish the old Sandringham Hall. A last resistance was mounted by the Prince – he stipulated that Teulon's chimneys must be retained. In the end the Prince had to be content with replicas. One can sense Humbert exercising a noble restraint when dealing with his exacting Royal client who considered that a new mansion could be built round existing chimney-stacks! The Princess demanded that her small sitting-room be left unchanged and she got her wish.

1865   *Illustrated London News*

A ball at Holkham Hall, Norfolk, given by Lord Leicester in honour of the Prince and Princess of Wales.

Compromisingly Humbert agreed to store the unused materials from Teulon's picturesque old entrance porch dating back to the Cowpers' occupancy, when replacing it by a *porte-cochère,* giving more cover. Many of these materials were later used in the building of the new ballroom in 1881-3.[11] Humbert also promised to keep Teulon's conservatory (it is still there though much modified), and to build an American bowling-alley alongside. 'The Prince's whole interest is taken up in the construction of the new bowling alley', noted Knollys. 'He is anxious it should eclipse that at Trentham [the Duke of Sutherland's Staffordshire seat], from which he borrowed the idea – everything else seems of minor importance.'[12] The bowling-alley, built at right angles, terminated in a projection closely matching Teulon's conservatory in style and materials. The builders were Goggs of Swaffham, who were widely experienced in erecting the brick and carstone buildings so typical of this part of Norfolk. The demolition and rebuilding was to take the best part of three years.

In 1869 the Prince rented near-by Gunton Hall for his usual Christmas visit to Norfolk, but over the New Year visits of 1865 to 1868 and in 1870 (that of 1869 being spent abroad), the Royal party were guests at Holkham Hall, seat of the Earl of Leicester.

After visiting Trentham Park, Staffordshire, the Prince of Wales instructed Humbert to build a bowling-alley at right angles to Teulon's conservatory. The alley was converted into a library in 1901.

Present at Holkham Hall in 1870 on the fifth visit was Annie, the younger daughter of Sir Anthony de Rothschild (1810-76), the Prince's financial adviser. Her father and her elder sister Constance, who later became Lady Battersea were also present. Annie has left some written comments on the Prince and Princess as guests. On the arrival of the Royal party at Holkham in December 1869 Annie writes: 'the two little boys [Prince Albert Victor and Prince George] toddled in first with great self-possession, followed by the Princess who looked very charming, and His Royal Highness, evidently in an excellent temper. . . . ' A few days later: 'We had a lovely day yesterday, very cold and very bright; all the gentlemen went at an early hour to business but the ladies were lazy and would not go out before lunch. The Princess appeared at 1 o'clock, looking charming in a short black velvet costume. In the afternoon those least humane, including myself, drove to see the gentlemen shooting; the poor pheasants rose in the air in such numbers that they quite blackened the sky and tumbled about all around us.'[13]

E. Bullock *c.* 1870

Builders no more kept to their dates a century ago than they do today, and at one time it looked as though the new house would not even be ready by the next Christmas – that of 1870.* Darkly the Prince muttered that the labourers' dinner, customarily given in the coach-house on his birthday – 9 November – would not be held. But he relented when the day came and Sandringham House turned out to be miraculously habitable; the men received a distribution of beef, bread and cheese, beer, and the ingredients of plum-pudding to take home.

'The new house seems quite charming, a very great improvement on the old one, and nicely furnished. It is warm and very comfortable, and feels quite dry', noted old 'Uncle George', the Duke of Cambridge. [14]

The Prince of Wales had taken advice on fireproofing, as we shall see later, and also on sanitation. The most modern installations were introduced at Sandringham, the work being carried out under the supervision of Thomas Crapper, the plumber, who was the real inventor of the modern cistern. [15] Previously control of the flow was by valves and much water was wasted.

The east front of Sandringham House by Humbert shortly after completion in 1870.

* *The Norfolk Chronicle* records the Prince and Princess staying at Sandringham for one night only following their opening of new docks at King's Lynn on 7 July 1869.

W. McLean 1870

The new Sandringham was described as a 'solidly built house in Salvin's manner but lacking in just that touch of distinction which marks most of Salvin's work'.[16] There were numerous examples of Anthony Salvin's work in Norfolk, had the Prince wished to see them, but the nearest, North Runcton Hall (now demolished) was one of his less inspired creations. Queen Victoria, when she first saw Sandringham House in 1871, thought it handsome.

The first house-party was held on 9 December 1870, the Prince considerately inviting the former owner, Spencer Cowper, who was doubtless pleased to see his old conservatory still standing though in its new guise as a billiard-room.

The west front of Sandringham House in 1870 showing Teulon's conservatory, now a billiard-room, and the bowling-alley backing on to it.

4
A tour of the new House

The eastern wall of the Great Saloon. This early view of 1889 shows the central gasolier before its modification for electricity.

THE NORFOLK HOME of the Prince and Princess of Wales was essentially a private one. Apart from their family, close friends, and carefully selected guests Sandringham House remained closed to the public gaze. However by comparing contemporary photographs and magazine articles it is possible to obtain some impression of what the House was like.

An article in *The World* of the mid 1870s states: 'In the inner wall of the vestibule above the hall door is set a tablet bearing this inscription in Old English characters: "This house was built by Albert Edward, Prince of Wales, and Alexandra, his wife, in the year of Our Lord 1870." The home savour of Sandringham begins from the very doorstep, for there is no formal entrance hall. The vestibule is simply part and parcel of the great saloon.' As we read the quaint room by room description of the house it is useful to compare it with some excellent photographs taken in 1889 by Bedford Lemere,[1] and with others published in *Country Life* in 1902.

Illustrations show a handsome archway of weapons and prominent candelabra-type gasoliers in the hall/saloon, as the main room was

Hudson and Kearns 1901   *Country Life*   Hudson and Kearns 1901   *Country Life*

indifferently called. The Prince was extremely proud of manufacturing his
own gas, as we have noted, and the article confirms that 'this noble
apartment has a lofty room of open oak work; its walls are covered with
pictures; and its area is almost encumbered with cosy chairs, occasional
tables, pictures on easels, musical instruments, flowers in stands, flowers
in pots, flowers in vases, and a thousand and one pretty trifles, each one
of which has an association and a history linked to it.' The later pictures
published in *Country Life* illustrate how little the Royal couple had wished
to change their surroundings in twelve years. Although there is a huge
brown bear standing on his hind legs, a Chillingham bull shot by the King,
and a 'pathetic portrait of the late Duke of Clarence and the present
Prince of Wales in their midshipmen's uniforms'.[2]

The Great Saloon, sometimes named as the Hall,
from the north and the south in 1901. Dances
were held in this fine galleried room until the
erection of the ballroom in 1881-84. The room is
now considerably lightened in tone.

B. Lemere 1889

Reproduced by gracious permission of Her Majesty the Queen

B. Lemere 1889

Reproduced by gracious permission of Her Majesty the Queen

'From the saloon opens the business room, occupied by General Sir William Knollys, the Comptroller . . . in this room it is where the Prince transacts his correspondence.' Sixty years later in 1932 King George V was to broadcast to the nation from this same room. In the years between 'a plain room, furnished in a plain and business-like style' appears to have changed little. The fine arched mirror, table candle lamps, comfortable leather-studded settee and chairs fill the library, 'a pleasant room in blue and light oak', which already in 1889 had expanded into a second room.

The second library 'opens into the vestibule of the garden entrance, which by reason of its proximity to the drawing room is always used on ball nights. From the main corridor stretching to the great staircase there opens on the right the principal reception rooms, but before these are reached there is passed the Prince's private morning room, a family room pure and simple. The admixture of feminine and masculine tastes of which this pretty room is, more than any other in the house, an example, speaks eloquently of lives blended in accord of close-knit domesticity. The walls, of cool neutral tint, are partly decorated with rare china and pottery, partly panelled with crayon pictures of deer-stalking episodes in the Highlands by the most celebrated English painters of our day. A large windowed projection, which is in part a lounge, in part a boudoir and in

The Prince of Wales's business-room in 1889, mainly used by his Comptrollers, first Sir William Knollys and then Sir Dighton Probyn.

The Prince of Wales's Morning Room in 1889, where he usually breakfasted alone.

part a writing room, is half partitioned off from the rest of the apartments by a screen devoted to the display of photographs.' These were undoubtedly Princess Alexandra's contribution; she greatly regretted the loss of so many snapshots in the Sandringham fire of 1891 – their absence is revealed in a photograph of the same room taken in 1901. 'A truss of tree-mignonette, with lilies of the valley blossoming around the bushy stem, half hides the panel on which Leighton's brush has depicted "The bringing the deer home"; the spreading skin of a huge tiger shot by the Prince in India lies on a quilt carpet of patchwork.'

'There are three drawing rooms, two small ones and a large one. They are all connected with the entrance hall by a broad corridor, which is ornamented by pieces of armour, ancient china, stuffed birds, etc.'

The ante-room of the Great Drawing Room is 'a pretty little apartment in French grey, having for its chief ornament a large picture of the Emperor of Russia* and the Prince. The principal drawing room looks out on to the park . . . it is a room of fine proportions, of whose walls the prevalent tint is a pale salmon colour; and its fixed decorations are studiously simple . . . merely a few mirrors placed panel-wise. . . . '[3] 'The various drawing rooms of which the particularly handsome ceilings are a marked feature . . . are full of evidence of the personal tastes of Queen Alexandra, whose portrait by Edward Hughes is their proudest ornament.' Mr Hughes was no Gainsborough, but in the production of what may be called 'pleasing family likenesses he is without rival'. The Royal couple preferred

This wide corridor, hung with trophies, was approached from the entrance portico on the eastern front and ran north and south, almost the whole length of the new Sandringham House, giving entrance to the main rooms on the ground floor.

Two smaller rooms lead into the Great Drawing Room. This one, by 1889, was already filled with innumerable *objets d'art*. The veneered bookcase with gilt-bronze mounts was executed by Holland and Sons. The porcelain in the recessed case is of German and Danish origin.

* Alexander II of Russia (born 1818; succeeded 1855; assassinated 1881) was the father-in-law both of the Prince's brother Alfred and of Princess Alexandra's sister Dagmar. He paid a State Visit to England in 1874.

    Country Life

'those pictures which have association to those which have merely artistic merit', such as the marriage of Prince Charles of Denmark, the Queen's father, and one of the many portraits of Queen Victoria by Winterhalter.

The Royal couple had collected Danish as well as the more fashionable Dresden china. Present also were 'little green frogs with ruby eyes, dogs' heads and jewelled heads for umbrellas or parasols'. Countless white elephants and pigs 'were spread through the drawing rooms'.[4] It is likely that some of these items so casually recorded in 1902 were part of the great collection of jewellery by Peter Carl Fabergé (1846-1920), the Russian Court Jeweller, which Queen Alexandra built up at Sandringham, where it remains to this day. 'Queen Alexandra was the sister of the Dowager Empress Marie Feodorovna and it was largely through the relationship of two Danish princesses that the custom grew of finding a small animal carving in natural stone, or a flower study poised in a rock crystal pot which appears, by a stratagem of the lapidary, to be filled with water, to add to the collection at Sandringham House. . . . The Sandringham collec-

The south end of the Great Drawing Room in 1889 and 1901. In twelve years many cluttered objects have disappeared. Without the Royal ladies' pictures the end wall seems unfinished in the earlier picture but the plasterwork, carpets, curtains, and palms appear unchanged.

B. Lemere   Reproduced by gracious permission of Her Majesty the Queen

Hudson and Kearns 1901   *Country Life*

The northern end of the Great Drawing Room in 1889 and 1901. *Cupid binding Venus' eyes* by the Italian sculptor Villa and the frames of photographs were especial favourites of the Princess of Wales.

tions . . . are . . . objects belonging to the beautiful Queen Alexandra, no longer, then, a young woman during the decade when she was Queen [1901-10] . . . It was on visits to Russia that King Edward VII and Queen Alexandra saw objects from Fabergé's workshops and conceived a taste for them. Later, King Edward fell a victim to the Russian habit and commissioned presents, yearly, for Queen Alexandra.'[5]

'The long vista of the bowling alley, lighted from both sides and roof, with raised seats at the upper end, whence ladies may look down on the tournament of their squires' discloses a building deliberately formed in the style of Teulon's conservatory in the old house, serving as the billiard-room of the 1870 mansion.'[6] By 1902 we read '... The favourite room in the house is the library. In days gone by it was the bowling alley . . . The wall of this delightful room opposite the windows is completely lined with well selected and well bound books, far and away the best adornment that can be given to any room . . . the family spend a great deal of time in it. Canon Hervey, the Rector of Sandringham [1878-1907] performs the duties of librarian . . . and in the centre of the great book shelves which

B. Lemere

Reproduced by gracious permission of Her Majesty the Queen

The Dining Room at Sandringham in 1889 after the gift of the Spanish tapestries by King Alfonso XII of Spain in 1876. The large panel of a wedding procession is by Goya.

B. Lemere

The Dining Room laid out for a banquet in 1889.

B. Lemere

The Library in 1889. Shortly after his accession in 1901, King Edward VII provided additional shelving in the former bowling-alley. 'The Library looked imposing, but while there were many valuable and interesting books it was mainly filled with trash, masses of presentation books in beautiful bindings, but quite unreadable. King Edward soon revolutionized this and cleared out all the rubbish. Mr Humphreys from Hatchard's shop in London came down and was told to supply books suitable for a country-house library.'[8]

line the side of the room is a little box containing tickets to be filled up by visitors who may wish to borrow books, with an accompanying table of instructions, for the King is remarkably methodical. . . .[7]

'In suite with the drawing room is the dining room . . . a great bow window expands from the centre of its front.' A dozen years on, Bedford Lemere's picture shows the room dignified with the Spanish tapestries given to the Prince by King Alfonso of Spain in 1876, just after the article we are quoting was written, and naturally much changed.

Lemere's interesting series illustrates only the first of two of the most significant rooms in the mansion; the 'beautiful [upstairs] room' is surely the sitting-room that the Princess had insisted on having reconstructed in every respect as it had been in the old house.

Not illustrated is the 'big comfortable home-like chamber, whither through the open door comes the song of the linnets in the Princess's dressing room', wherein 'a strong man . . . battled for breath' – an allusion, of course, to the Prince's near-fatal illness of 1871. We are invited to gaze in awe on 'the hole bearing a hook, supporting the trapeze

Princess Alexandra had insisted that her room in the new house be a replica of that in the old and Humbert obliged.

. . . by which the Prince, when on the slow and weary road to convalescence, was wont to change his recumbent position or pull himself up into a sitting position.'[9]

The World leaves to later writers a description of the Princess's bedroom 'fantastically crowded with photographs, holy pictures, little crosses and mementoes of every sort and kind. By her bedside she always kept a small replica of Thorwaldsen's statue of Christ; over her bed, in the angle of the curtains draping the bed head, the carved head of a cherub hung above a large crucifix'.[10]

The bathrooms of the Prince and Princess were identical except that his bath was black and hers white, each was made of marble and illumined by gas.[11]

1902

Lafayette

THE SOCIAL LIFE at Sandringham ranged from the rigid formality of a visit from a Head of State such as those of 1881, 1899, and 1902 by Kaiser Wilhelm II to the complete informality of the Royal Family alone in the House and enjoying themselves. Between these extremes there was the country-house week-end party when the Prince and Princess of Wales would arrive with their guests at Wolferton Station and drive through the two miles of pine-clad heathland to the House.

Three times a year there was a ball. The following extract taken from a letter written by Louisa Caroline Buxton, Mayoress of Norwich, to her widowed sister Anna Maria Reynolds Mackinnes from Cranmer Hall, Fakenham, where she and the Mayor, Samuel Gurney Buxton, were staying as guests of Sir Willoughby Jones so as to be within reasonable reach of Sandringham, some sixteen miles distant, illustrates vividly one such ball held at Sandringham House on 2 December 1873. Nothing points more to that remoteness desired by Queen Victoria and Prince Albert for their son's country-house than the fact that the Mayor and Mayoress of Norwich could not, a hundred years ago, attend the Royal couple at Sandringham direct from their own country seat of Catton Hall.

'I preferred eating to sleeping this morning and came down to breakfast with Gurney* soon after 10 before he started hunting, the meet being near Sandringham. The rest of the world – Jones and Lombes – now breakfasting 11.40. Well I must begin at the beginning. We dined at 6 and

Kaiser Wilhelm II of Germany visiting his uncle's country home in 1902. Previous visits were in 1881 and 1899.

5

A visit to the 'Big House'

* Her husband, the Mayor, who did not use his first name of Samuel.

1862   *Illustrated London News*

dressed afterwards and started at a quarter to nine. My dress was decidedly one of the prettiest at the Ball . . . it is a *very* good satin with nothing however – excepting a very little white satin, but my own lace. It had a deep flounce round the bottom. So mad: Kennet (of London) *is* expensive; we each went in our own carriage (i.e. the Jones' and the Buxtons) and ours being lighted and warmed we were well provided for the drive. My story book was left behind wh[ich] was the only contre-temps. The greater part of the way was over very bad roads so we did not get to Sandringham until 10.30 – We found crowds arriving. The Prince and Princess had just come in and the Dancing had just begun so we went through no sort of introduction and I did not see either for about 20 minutes.

'The plan was that the Jones' were invited and requested to give in the names of the friends they were going to bring – so that they might be approved first. We entered through a corridor – like a passage to a church at a wedding – on entering and through a small hole to the large hall where the dancing was. This was longer but not so wide as our Library [at Catton] – Gurney thought it was not on the whole quite so large. It was high up to the roof and fitted with oak – There was a gallery at one end and also two little galleries filled all the evening with maids – the larger gallery was only inhabited by a little negro boy who was grinning and rolling his eyes with delight. He appears in that picture of the children which was in the exhibition this year and which hung over the doorway

The road to Sandringham. In the distance is a train making its way to Wolferton Station.

Great Eastern Railway Magazine

The road to Sandringham from Wolferton Station through the pine and heathland.

Norfolk County Libraries

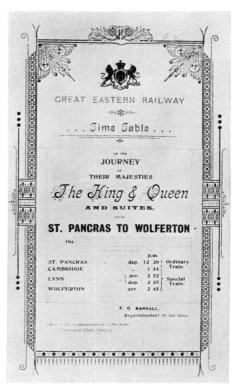

Great Eastern Railway Magazine

King Edward VII and Queen Alexandra leaving Wolferton Station for Sandringham.

An example of a Royal timetable:
On 12 August 1867 Sir William Knollys wrote in his Diary: 'I went with the prince to Sandringham. We had a new route by Peterborough; . . . ordinary train there and special to Lynn and Wolferton. 3 hrs K[ing's] X to Wolferton.'[7]

leading into the drawing room – Over the fireplace was a picture of the Princess and the King and Queen of Denmark [her parents], on each side. The windows had brilliant red curtains which looked very well – They were measurably open all the evening so it was never hot. We slowly made our way up the room – meeting friends on the way – Gurdons – Hamonds, Lee Warners etc. All the ladies in their best diamonds – Lady Walsingham, a little withered old lady, was a perfect mass of them. At the further end of the hall was the Princess – there she remained all the evening, only moving for supper – she was dressed in a not *very* pretty blue dress – satin tunic with deep lace round it over blue tulle "ornaments pearls and diamonds" – the latter sprinkled over her chignon – She looked as pale as possible – not nearly so pretty as at the rink. . . .

'There were not many *very* great swells and she did not dance much – she moved a little way out of her corner to talk to some ladies, but mostly she kept with the two or three very select ones – the Countess Gleichen being the grandest – so they weren't anything *very* particular. The Duchess of Manchester in primrose satin was there enammelled [*sic*] all over face and neck – I may say back – for like the poor beggars she was "half naked to behold" – Lady Blandford in pale green and lace was very pretty. Mrs. Grey in yellow – not at all what I fancied her from her book* – and two or three others. The Prince looked fat and bald but very smiling and sociable – He went about all over the room, dancing all the evening. It was very entertaining to see the ladies making their low curtsies when he asked them or spoke to them – otherwise he passed about as an ordinary gentleman – he did not dance with Rosie† – but though she looked very pretty, there were such a *very* large number of pretty and beautiful faces that she was not particularly noticeable.

'Lady Boileau looked perfect in pink satin and lace and diamonds. I found a charming little corner where I had a comfortable, though rather draughty seat and could see about me – I was just opposite where the Princess was sitting – The Duke of Cambridge was there and danced close by me one Lancers when I was dancing so that I had a splendid opportunity of really *examining* the "George" – There were several bestarred gentlemen. . . . After I was tired of watching the dancing (I only danced 3 dances) I went into the Drawing rooms which were exceedingly pretty – beautifully furnished and full of comfortable armchairs and sofas. Also endless photograph books – 2 of which I looked through. One was very interesting all of the Princess and her sisters and brothers very old ones – looking oh so dowdy! in the costumes of – say – nursery governesses – but with such pleasant simple faces – The little girl "Thyra" principally attired in checks and plaids. In one of the drawing rooms there were 2 exquisite groups in marble – so there was plenty to be amused with besides lots of friends. Rosie did not like it so much as I did – and I do not think it was so amusing for *quite* young ladies for there was rather a lack of gentlemen and the dancing was necessarily formal.

'At about one the greatest swells went into the dining room to supper – the door was shut on them and they gourmandized for such a long time that we all got not a little hungry. When we did get in we found a most recherché supper – There was soup and hot dishes (salmi of woodcock amongst them) but I had cold savoury jellies and lobster salad with cockscombs and all sorts of little dainties – I did not mention that in a library through the drawing room tea etc. was going on all the evening. We had heard that it would not be etiquette to go away until Royalty retired but the carriages were ordered at 1.30 – so at about 2.30 people began to go – and we left at about 3. We had a slow drive home, not getting back till after five but I slept a good part of the time and did not mind it. It was altogether a most amusing and particularly pretty sight and quite came up to my expectations. They *must* have done breakfast by this time. So I must go. Most affectionately, L. C. Buxton. P.S. the dining room was a beautiful room with pictures of the royal sisters and brothers all round in panels.'[2]

Norfolk County Libraries

Wolferton waiting-rooms. The first Royal waiting-rooms were not built until 1876, yet a set on the opposite platform had to be built in 1898, by which time the traffic for Sandringham was so great that the line had had to be doubled.

Norfolk County Libraries

The interior of the Royal waiting-room at Wolferton Station photographed in 1914.

* Maria Georgina Grey (1816-1906) known as Mrs William Grey, with her unmarried sister Emily Shirreff, was a pioneer of women's rights. The book Louisa refers to was probably *The Education of Women* (1871). The other ladies from outside Norfolk referred to were the current leaders of Society.

† Rosalind Buxton, *née* Upcher, the wife of Gurney's brother Henry, of Fritton Hall, Great Yarmouth. Her husband did not attend the ball, so she was in her brother-in-law's party.

There is much of interest in this letter. Many of the people entertained were Norfolk neighbours of the Buxtons. It is significant that in the hegemony of the landed gentry even so notable a personage as the Mayor of Norwich had to be vouched for by a landowner. The little Negro boy on the gallery was Ali Achmet whom Princess Alexandra had brought from Nubia during her Eastern tour of 1868-69. Princess Thyra was Princess Alexandra's youngest sister who eventually became the Duchess of Cumberland. Louisa was three months pregnant at the age of thirty-three when she wrote this letter and was to live only a further six years.

Some guests had perforce to confine themselves to indoor occupations for the Prince would only allow his guests to shoot if he thought they were capable. Guests would read, write letters, sketch in the grounds, or play whist. The Royal couple did not put in an appearance in the morning, so they were free from restraint. Dancing was not always on the programme and as the years passed plays became popular.

Disraeli paid his first visit to Sandringham a day or two after this ball on 6 December 1873. Writing to Lady Chesterfield on 15 December he said: 'I was agreeably disappointed with Sandringham. It is not commonplace – both wild and stately. I fancied I was paying a visit to some of the dukes and princesses of the Baltic; a vigorous marine air, stunted fir forests, but sufficiently extensive, the roads and all appurtenances on a great scale, and the splendour of Scandinavian sunsets.' [3]

Gladstone had been at Sandringham in 1872 but his happiest visit was in 1880 when the Gladstone Papers, quoted by Battiscombe, tell us that the Princess tucked his wife up on the last night.* When he spent a further week-end on the estate in 1883 the village grocer, deputizing at the Sunday morning service for the usual organist, played atrociously.

Constance, Lady Battersea (*née* Rothschild), also recorded a visit to Sandringham in its early days. In January 1874 she and her father, Sir Anthony de Rothschild, the Prince's financial adviser, were visitors along with Disraeli, and the Sunday sermon by Dr Magee, Bishop of Peterborough (later Archbishop of York) offended one or two of those present by its reference to idle youth (*jeunesse dorée*). The day passed with Princess Alexandra singing hymns after tea, and just when everyone was ready for bed the Prince took out his watch and said 'Sunday being over we may resort to the bowling alley.' Princess Alexandra's conversation was mainly about her sister Princess Dagmar, now the Grand Duchess Marie Feodorovna of Russia, who with her husband, the future Emperor Alexander III of Russia (1845-94), had visited England some six months earlier. When Constance Rothschild was eventually able to retire, the Princess personally escorted her to her room and lit her candles. [5]

Reproduced by gracious permission of Her Majesty the Queen

An oil-painting by Heinrich von Angeli of the Prince and Princess of Wales with two of their children, Prince Albert Victor, later Duke of Clarence, and Princess Maud, later Queen of Norway. In the distance behind Prince Albert Victor can be seen Sandringham House. The picture hangs in the Great Saloon.

* Colonel Francis Knollys, the Comptroller's son who had become the Prince's Private Secretary, did not share the Princess's enthusiasm for Mrs Gladstone, describing her as 'gushing and ridiculous to the last degree' in 1872. [4]

1907

Many years later King Edward VII's Assistant Private Secretary somewhat cynically described the social activities at Sandringham House. 'The guests had to do something or say they were doing something, as the King liked to think all his guests were being amused. It was quite enough to say "I am going to watch the golf" . . . but unless some answer was given the King though out some amusement which really bored the guests stiff. . . . Tea was a full-dress meal with all the women in tea gowns and the men in short black jackets and black ties. Gottlieb's band played like a bee in a bottle for an hour. Then everyone played games but those who knew the routine tiptoed off to the library and read or talked. Dinner was magnificent with all the women in tiaras, etc. and all the men with ribands and decorations. Bridge had just become the fashion and the King walked round to see that everyone was engaged. The Queen went to bed soon after midnight and the King between one and one thirty.'[6]

Yet the House did not strike the guest as ostentatious. 'Apart from the Goya tapestries (a gift from King Alphonso of Spain) which looked down on the dining-table, there was scarcely an item in the whole building which would strike the visitor's eye as unmistakably regal. Indeed had the visitor wandered in by chance, had he not looked closely enough at some of the faces and signatures on the photographs; had he not perceived that those toy figures of animals were not trinkets from a parish bazaar but Fabergé creations sent by the Tzar of all the Russians he might well have thought he had strayed into the showpiece mansion of some Midlands industrialist

A house-party at Sandringham on 6 November 1907. King Edward VII invariably spent 9 November, his birthday, at Sandringham. All members of the house-party took their lunch with the guns.

rather than into the country seat of a future king. In the clothes they wore both the Prince of Wales and his bride imposed their very personal and basically simple tastes upon the world of fashion around them . . . Yet a true home it was. . . . One of the main reasons for this was a sense of almost childish fun which pervaded every corner of the cluttered house. The Prince was something of a prankster all his life. . . . The ballroom was turned in wet weather into an area for tricycle races, and the grand staircase was often converted with the aid of a large silver tray, into a carpeted toboggan run.'[7]

Practical jokes characterized many an occasion. The Prince of Wales enjoyed seeing his guests happy in an uproarious way and often indulged in horseplay. His three daughters, then in their late teens, also enjoyed the artless jokes that their father encouraged. Making apple-pie beds, dousing beds with water, or putting dead animals or birds under the bedclothes are incidents related by guests of the period. Unfortunately some guests went much further than was desirable or proper. One forward guest released Charlie – one of two bears which the Prince had acquired on his travels – from the bear pit he occupied in the grounds causing a great alarm. Then on 1 April 1883 – All Fools' Day – when the Prime Minister, W. E. Gladstone, was lunching privately with the Prince, a joker invited prominent politicians from all over North Norfolk to join them.[8]

The principal activity at Sandringham was, of course, shooting. The Prince had no ambition to become a first-class shot but he liked being out of doors as much as possible. Because of shooting the clocks were permanently advanced by half an hour. This was to make the maximum possible use of daylight. The practice was copied from the Earl of Leicester at Holkham Hall. The Prince 'liked a high partridge and a rocketing pheasant but derived his principal enjoyment from the fresh air and exercise, and from seeing everybody around him as happy and carefree as himself'.[9]

Louisa Cresswell the tenant of Appleton House, on the estate, although antagonistic towards the disruption caused by the shooting has left a graphic account: 'A complete silence having been secured for miles around the day [is] ushered in by a procession of boys with blue and pink flags, like a Sunday School treat, a band of gamekeepers in green and gold with the head man on horseback, an army of beaters in smocks and hats bound with Royal red, a caravan for the reception of the game and a tailing off of loafers to see the fun, for H.R.H. is very good-natured in allowing people to look in on his amusements provided they do not interfere with them, and if it could be conveniently arranged would perhaps have no objection to everybody's life being skittles and beer, like his own.

Radio Times Hulton Picture Library

King Edward VII shooting at Sandringham.

W. J. Edward 1908

'At about 11 o'clock the Royal party arrive in a string of waggonettes, and range themselves in a long line under the fences or behind the shelters put up for that purpose, each sportsman having loaders in attendance with an extra gun or guns to hand backwards and forwards, to load and reload. The boys and beaters are stationed in a semi-circle some distance off and it is their place to beat up the birds and drive them to the fences, the waving flags frightening them from flying back. On they come in ever increasing numbers until they burst in a cloud over the fence where the guns are concealed. This is the exciting moment, a terrific fusillade ensues, birds dropping down in all directions, wheeling about in confusion between the flags and the guns, the survivors gathering themselves together and escaping into the fields beyond. The shooters then retire to another line of fencing, making themselves comfortable with camp stools and cigars until the birds are driven up as before, and so through the day, only leaving off for luncheon in a tent brought down from Sandringham, or in very cold weather it is carried into the nearest house.'[10]

King Edward VII shooting partridge at Shernborne.

A skating party with the Prince and Princess of Wales on the frozen Sandringham lake in 1908. With them are their four growing children, Prince Henry, Prince Edward, Prince Albert, and Princess Mary. Holding up Prince Henry is Henry Peter Hansell, the Royal children's tutor.

After the day's shooting guests retired to the 'Big House', or to the Bachelors' Cottage, or to the outlandish Folly designed by C. S. Beck. Often in these winter months the lake in front of the House was frozen over and there were 'the evening skating parties [which] stand out as a scene of fairytale enchantment, the lake, the island illuminated with coloured lamps and torches, the skating chairs with glow worm lights and the skaters flitting past and disappearing in the darkness'.[11]

The annual head shot increased from some 7,000 to close on 30,000 between 1870 and 1910. The Prince of Wales preferred partridge to pheasant-shooting, but in the last year of his life only 411 partridge were shot at Sandringham, and on one of his last days out with the guns the King said to his Head Keeper, 'Thank you Jackson. If it had not been for the pheasants, I should have had nothing for my guests.'[12]

As Prince of Wales he had been to Hungary early in the 1880s with Jackson to learn the *remise* system thoroughly. It was most useful in open country both for breeding and for driving. Small enclosures ranged in enclaves of some acres in extent grouped together alternate plantings of buckwheat, mustard, and gorse. The eggs were thinned out as hatching approached, and the enclosures protected the birds from overlaying their young. On one of the later shoots at Sandringham, the King asked that no female birds should be shot, but one of his colleagues, Sir Somerville Gurney did not hear the request, and brought down a hen. Rather than rebuke him publicly, the King said, 'Ah, Gurney, what a man you are for the ladies!', whereupon Sir Somerville took the point, and immediately apologized.[13]

IN 1871 THE YEAR after the new house was completed the Prince lost his sixth child and third son, Prince Alexander, who lived for only one day. The Prince himself suffered an extremely serious attack of typhoid fever which led Queen Victoria to pay her first visit to Sandringham. For those attending the Queen the visit sometimes proved more of an ordeal than a pleasure. Her Majesty had definite views as to when members of her household might or might not be available, and one day when she appeared unexpectedly a group of courtiers had hurriedly to hide themselves in a clump of bushes until she had gone by.

A few days later after leaving Sandringham the Queen had to make a hasty return when the Prince's condition worsened and there was very serious concern for his life. To the relief of the Queen and the nation the Prince survived and made a slow recovery.

From the immense public sadness of that year as recorded there remains what have been termed the two worst lines of English verse. They were perpetrated by the Poet Laureate Alfred Austin (1835-1913) and expressed the anxiety felt by the nation during the Prince's fluctuating illness:

> Across the wires the electric message came
> He is no better; he is much the same.

With his recovery the Prince of Wales returned happily to the building or improving of cottages on the estate and after Sunday luncheon he delighted in showing off the latest improvements to his guests. In 1877, in view of the prevalence of typhoid, the Prince built a new waterworks a mile from Sandringham House at Appleton – on the site of a spring which (according to the weather) yielded from 15,000 to 150,000 gallons daily. Martin Folkes designed an elegant Italianate-style water-tower which held 32,000 gallons of water. It stands 121 feet above Sandringham House.

That same year General Sir William Knollys, the Prince's first Comptroller retired. He was succeeded by Sir Dighton Probyn, who held the office from 1877 to 1891. In the 1880s the Prince added some additional rooms for the Comptroller and Equerries – and a small post office which remained in use until 1968.

Three balls were held annually: for the gentry; for the farmers; and for the servants. In 1881 the Prince celebrated his fortieth birthday by adding a ballroom to Sandringham. Previously balls had been held in the Saloon The Prince's Architect, Humbert, had died in 1877 at the age of forty-five. *The Builder* tells us of a visit to the Isle of Man in a vain attempt to restore his health and of a 'delicate sense of honour, and a somewhat reticent and reserved manner which concealed a kind and generous disposition'.[1] The Norfolk architect Robert W. Edis (1839-1927) was selected to succeed

1871   *Illustrated London News*

In November 1871 the Prince of Wales appeared to be on the point of death at Sandringham House. Queen Victoria had not previously visited her son and daughter-in-law in their country home, and is shown on 29 November being met by her second son Prince Alfred at Wolferton Station. The outcrop of rock in the background is artistic licence.

6

Albert Edward Prince of Wales

1870-1901

W. and D. Donney

Radio Times Hulton Picture Library

The Prince of Wales's Family

King Edward VII
1841-1910

Queen Alexandra
1844-1925

Albert Victor
Duke of Clarence
1864-1892

King George V
1865-1936

Louise
Princess Royal
1867-1931

Victoria
1868-1935

Maud
Queen of Norway
1869-1938

Alexander
born and died
1871

Albert Edward, Prince of Wales, as Grand Master of the United Grand Lodge of England, the Head of English Freemasonry, which post he held from 1875 until his accession to the Throne in 1901. He was an active member of the Provincial Grand Lodge of Norfolk, under whose jurisdiction Sandringham House fell, and participated on four occasions in Masonic ceremonies in the Province.

F. Frith 1896 · Norfolk County Libraries   F. Frith 1927 · Norfolk County Libraries

Humbert, probably on the recommendation of one of the Prince's neighbours.

Edis subsequently made his name with the building of the Great Central Hotel at Marylebone, and of the Inner Temple Library. He attained the Presidency of the Architects' Association and settled down at the Old Hall, Ormesby, Norfolk. Later he was knighted, became a Commander of the Bath, and was a Deputy Lieutenant for the county before his long life came to a close. Edis's ballroom was completed in 1884. It measured sixty-six feet by thirty feet and was lighted by large bay-windows,[2] the whole being crowned with a roof turret. Some of Teulon's materials, held in store since the porch was demolished, were brought into use again for the mouldings of the ballroom entrance porch. The Prince could now hold balls without encroaching on the privacy of his house.

In January 1885 there was celebrated at Sandringham the coming-of-age of the Royal couple's eldest son, Prince Albert Victor, who in 1890 was created Duke of Clarence and Avondale. In the family circle he was known as 'Prince Eddy' or even more familiarly as 'collars and cuffs', the latter appellation referred to his rather elongated neck and arms.

The young Prince was regaled with a special performance of 'Lord' George Sanger's Circus, the Big Top being set up in Sandringham Park. The day ended with an appearance of the comedian J. L. Toole in an

The Ballroom differed in style from Humbert's 1870 eastern front, which it partially obscures. However, it looks well from the main entrance, with a large Tudor-style window in its north face, and a turret-crowned entrance incorporating at the Prince's request some of the stones that had been removed from the old Sandringham Hall portico and carefully stored.

B. Lemere 1889

Inside the Ballroom built by the Prince to celebrate his fortieth birthday.

48

B. Lemere 1888   Reproduced by gracious permission of Her Majesty the Queen

The Princess of Wales (holding a dog), later Queen Alexandra, with her children in 1888. Behind her is Princess Maud (1869-1938), later Queen of Norway. Next to her is Princess Louise (1867-1931), afterwards Duchess of Fife and Princess Royal. Her eldest son, Albert Victor, Duke of Clarence (left), (1864-1892) died unmarried. On the right is Prince George (1865-1936), later Duke of York, Prince of Wales, and King George V. Her third daughter Princess Victoria (1868-1935), who never married, is not in the photograph.

B. Lemere 1889

By 1887 a large conservatory had been added next to the new Ballroom; this was later known as the 'Flower Court'.

entertainment in the new ballroom. The occasion was marked, we are told, by great rejoicings throughout the county. In Norwich the Mayor inviting 600 children to a Fancy Dress Ball at St Andrew's Hall to mark the event.

In 1887 a large conservatory was built adjoining the new ballroom and in 1888 the Prince and Princess of Wales celebrated their Silver Wedding. The following year Queen Victoria made her only formal visit to Sandringham.

Everything augured well for the Queen's visit. Her Golden Jubilee two years earlier had lightened some of the gloom which had enveloped the Queen since the death of the Prince Consort. The special Royal waiting-rooms at Wolferton Station which had been erected a decade earlier in 1876 were extensively decorated and the whole processional way to Sandringham was lined with triumphal arches. 'The station was very prettily decorated', wrote the Queen. 'The sun came out and all looked very bright. I got into Bertie's large landau, open, with four horses and postillions, and dear Alix insisted on sitting backwards with [her eldest

48

daughter Princess] Louise in order that I might be better seen. Bertie and Eddie rode on either side. . . .All was the same as that terrible time [1871: the year of the Prince's illness] and yet all is different.'

Members of the West Norfolk Hunt, headed by Sir Dighton Probyn, were present, many of them wearing hunting-pink. Encamped in Sandringham Park were a hundred men of the Norfolk Artillery who formed the Guard of Honour when the Queen drove through the Park on the following day. During her stay Her Majesty visited Castle Rising and several of the neighbouring villages.

On the last night of her visit the Queen indulged in one of her favourite pastimes – she witnessed theatricals in the new ballroom. Her Majesty rarely attended a performance in a public theatre but each of her residences was made to contain an improvised stage with room to accommodate the various properties. At Sandringham 'the stage was beautifully arranged, and with great scenic effects, and the pieces were splendidly mounted and with numbers of people taking part. I believe there were between sixty and seventy, as well as the orchestra.' Henry Irving and Ellen Terry were among the performers and were presented to the Queen.

In view of the complaints the Queen had made in 1871 all clocks were moved from Sandringham time to Greenwich Mean Time during her stay. And the time went well – 'we left Sandringham at half-past ten, having spent a very pleasant time under dear Bertie and Alix's roof, and I was greatly touched by all their kindness and affection', was the Queen's summing-up of her visit. [3]

It was natural enough that this summing-up should be slightly less than enthusiastic for the Queen had no real regard for Sandringham House, associated as it was with the terrible anxieties of December 1871 when she really believed at one stage that her eldest son would die on the tenth anniversary of his father's death and of the same terrible disease. And, of course, though Prince Albert had initiated the purchase of the old Sandringham Hall, his death in December 1861 had prevented his ever visiting it.

Naturally the Queen preferred to recall the happy hours with her husband at Osborne, her Isle of Wight home; or at Balmoral in the Scottish Highlands, residences where he had not only been at her side but where he had personally carried out much of the planning and equipping. Never again after 1889 was Queen Victoria to rest in the Royal waiting-rooms at Wolferton Station through which representatives of almost every Royal House in Europe were to pass on their way to visit their distinguished relatives, the Prince and Princess of Wales.

Alice Hughes 1889   Gernsheim Collection

The Princess of Wales in 1889.

50

B. Lemere 1889   Reproduced by gracious permission of Her Majesty the Queen

Prince George of Wales at twenty-four was
known mainly to the public as the companion of
his elder brother on their long voyages on the
corvette H.M.S. *Bacchante*. This picture of 1889
shows Princess Victoria, Prince George, Princess
Maud, the Hon. Winifred Sturt, and the Hon.
Julie Stonor.

In that same year of 1889 the Royal couple's eldest daughter Louise
married and two years later, on 17 May 1891 presented them with their
first grandchild named Alexandra after her grandmother. The Prince of
Wales was now forty-nine and Princess Alexandra forty-six. This happiness
was a small comfort for the year 1891 was to prove full of anxieties and
setbacks.

Earlier in the year the Prince had suffered the loss of Edmund Beck, his Agent at Sandringham. Then on 31 October after a very dry month, the disastrous fire broke out in the house. At about 7.30 p.m. the alarm was raised and well-rehearsed fire drills were put into operation immediately. As a result of the fire the whole of the top-floor bedrooms belonging to the Princesses were burnt out and the rooms of Charlotte Knollys, Fräulein Noedel, and several of the dressers were completely destroyed.[4] But the floors held, these having been strengthened earlier on the advice of Eyre Shaw (later Sir) the Head of the Metropolitan Fire Brigade. Some of the contents of the house were damaged by water and smoke but fortunately everything was fully insured.

Nevertheless, without Beck and with the inevitable disruption caused by the fire the Prince declared 'I shall pass my birthday [9 November] as arranged'[5] at Sandringham, which he did sheltered by tarpaulins.

A few days later Prince George, who had never given his parents a moment's anxiety, fell very ill indeed of typhoid. The Prince, recalling his father's death of the same illness in 1861, and his own attack of 1871, agonized at the bedside of his son. The Princess of Wales who, following a visit to her parents in Denmark, had gone on to her sister Marie, Empress of Russia, hurried back from the Royal Palace at Livadia arriving in England on 22 November to keep vigil at Prince George's side. Fortunately he had improved sufficiently for his parents to feel relieved delight at the engagement of their son and heir, Prince Albert Victor, Duke of Clarence to Princess Mary (May) of Teck, one day after his brother had been pronounced out of danger. This event took place at Luton Hoo in Bedfordshire.

A Royal party, including the Prince and Princess of Wales, and the Duke of York leaving Sandringham Church.

The Royal parents were particularly pleased about the Duke of Clarence's engagement, having been bitterly disappointed at their failure for religious and political reasons to bring to fruition an earlier romance with Princess Hélène d'Orléans, a Roman Catholic and daughter of the Comte de Paris, Pretender to the French Throne. Now in the 10th Hussars, the Prince was beginning to carry out public engagements. Often at Sandringham, where his childhood and youth had been spent, in May 1891 he opened a bazaar at Great Yarmouth in aid of the restoration of the Parish Church, and in November inaugurated a Trade and Industrial Exhibition at St James's Hall in King's Lynn.[6]

At the close of the year the Prince of Wales wrote from Sandringham to his widowed sister, the Empress Frederick of Germany: 'I cannot regret that the year '91 is about to close as, during it, I have experienced many worries and annoyances which ought to last me for a long time. My only happiness has been Eddy's engagement and Georgy's recovery.'[7]

Unhappily the greatest sadness was yet to come. On 8 January the Duke of Clarence celebrated his twenty-eighth birthday at Sandringham. His mother, his fiancée, his sister Victoria, and several of the entourage had bad colds, turning to a particularly virulent form of influenza which claimed him also. He took to his bed half-way through his birthday, unable even to attend the celebration dinner. Seven days later he died after a vigil kept by his fiancée and members of the family. Visitors can see the commemorative tablet on the east front marking the small bay-windowed room where a prince in direct line to the British Throne died on 14 January.

The *Norfolk Daily Standard* reported 'there is one more scene to chronicle, when all England mourned over his father's son taken away in early manhood and when the brightest of bright futures was opening out before him. To the chancel of the grey old church they bore the corpse . . . and thither father, mother, sisters and affianced bride went to calm their sorrows in prayer beside their loved one's coffin. Thither came the simple villagers of the district and others of nobler grade, simply to walk in quiet procession past the flower-covered coffin that lay before the altar, and to drop a tear for manhood early laid in the dust. It was not for him to rest there, for Royalty has its inexorable fashion in death as well as in life, and so he was borne to the railway station below in saddened pomp, to be whirled away over the iron road to the last resting-place of the Royal dead at Windsor.'

The Prince of Wales showed immense courage and resilience in the face of this great family tragedy. But the three annual balls for the gentry, for the farmers, and for the servants, were never regularly held again after 1891.

The Prince threw himself into repairing and indeed improving Sandringham House after the damage caused by the fire of 1891. He instructed Edis to introduce a whole line of store-rooms and staff bedrooms over Teulon's billiard-room and Humbert's bowling-alley, which the architect contrived with considerable skill. Edis had to copy the carstone of the earlier building although restrictions of weight confined him to constructing one additional storey. The final embellishment of the building of this period was a clock-tower over the ballroom, provided by the local tradesmen in memory of the Duke of Clarence.

The last decade before the Prince of Wales ascended the Throne as King Edward VII in 1901 saw the emergence of a second family residence on the Sandringham estate. In 1892 the direct line of succession was represented by Prince George, weakened by his recent illness, and unknown outside his family and Naval and Court circles. Should he, too, die the heiress

1893   Gernsheim Collection

A charming study of Princess May at Sandringham shortly after her marriage in 1893 to George, Duke of York. Her life included much sadness. Her first fiancé (the Duke of Clarence) died after six weeks' engagement. Of her five sons; the eldest (King Edward VIII) abdicated; the second (King George VI) died at fifty-six after much ill-health; the fourth (George, Duke of Kent) was killed on active service in 1942, and the fifth (John) died aged thirteen.

F. Frith 1897

Norfolk County Libraries

presumptive would be his eldest sister Princess Louise, who was married to the much older Duke of Fife. The Princess had one daughter, the infant Alexandra. While the Prince and Princess were still in deepest mourning it was decided that Prince George must marry. All ended happily for on 6 July 1893 Prince George married Princess May, just over a year after she had been expected to marry his brother. She was an ideal bride, her mother being the ebullient English princess, Mary Adelaide of Teck, who had always enjoyed her frequent visits to Sandringham.

It was perhaps rather surprising that the Prince of Wales gave his son the Bachelors' Cottage for use as a country home for it needed much alteration. Furthermore there were never enough guest-rooms in Sandringham House despite its great size. Possibly at the time no other reasonably secluded estate house was available. In any case the Prince's family was so closely united that it probably never occurred to Prince George, now Duke of York, that his wife might have no desire to live within five minutes' walk of her mother-in-law, nor spend her honeymoon in a house in which she was to live much of the time during the next thirty years. The Prince of Wales, the Duke of York, and his married sister, the Duchess of Fife selected the carpets, wallpapers, and furniture more than six months before the announcement of the Duke's engagement. For the Bachelors' Cottage had been assigned to him shortly after his brother's death and before his marriage had become an urgent constitutional necessity.

After the fire of 1891 the Prince of Wales introduced a long line of store-rooms and staff bedrooms with dormer-windows under a new roof-line. Edis skilfully built over Teulon's conservatory and Humbert's matching bowling-alley. The new additions gave Sandringham a 500 foot frontage, one of the longest in the country. After King Edward VII's improvements at the centre of this front in 1904 and the north end in 1909 Sandringham possessed 365 rooms, more than any other English private house.

Great Eastern Railway Magazine

An entrance ticket issued by the Great Eastern Railway to watch the Duke and Duchess of York leave Liverpool Street Station for Sandringham after their marriage on 6 July 1893.

1897   Reproduced by gracious permission of Her Majesty the Queen

1897   Reproduced by gracious permission of Her Majesty the Queen

1930

The Dining Room of York Cottage as originally furnished by Edis. After some years a new Dining Room was made in the extension farther along the lake, this room became a second drawing room. Soon after the death of Queen Victoria, when the Duke and Duchess of York became next in line to the Throne, consideration was given to leasing near-by Houghton Hall and giving up York Cottage. Queen Alexandra indicated that she liked having her family close at hand, and the idea was not pursued. [8]

The Drawing Room of York Cottage which looked out on to the lake and which was furnished by Maples on the Duke of York's instructions before he and his bride took up residence. The Duchess of York wrote in 1898: 'I do not quite like the incandescent gas and it seems so strong and hurts our eyes . . . we shall have to have shades on most of the burners in the living rooms.' [9]

York Cottage in 1930 showing the leaden pelican installed in 1898 on which the future Queen Mary commented 'the fountain Ferdy Rothschild gave is *hideous,* don't tell Mother dear [the Princess of Wales] . . . when Mackellar [the Head Gardener] turned on the water I roared with laughter at this truly ludicrous sight.' [10] The pelican's head alone is now visible, and he has long ceased to gush out water.

The Duke of York enjoying a sail on Sandringham lake in 1893 shortly after his marriage.

Some £5,000 was spent on improving York Cottage, as it came to be known, giving the Duke and Duchess a house which provided little privacy and was pervaded by constant cooking smells inside while outside it was 'all gables and hexagonal turrets and beams and tiny balconies'.[11]

Prince Edward (later Edward VIII) was born at White Lodge, Richmond Park, near London, on 23 June 1894. That same year had seen a tremendous gale at Sandringham. The Prince of Wales writing on 28 March states: 'We lost 2500 trees at Sandringham.'[12] Then in the following year on 14 December Sandringham was graced with the birth of the future British monarch, George VI, at York Cottage.

In 1896 the Prince of Wales enjoyed a most successful racing season. The Prince of Wales's later famous racing colours of purple, gold braid, scarlet sleeves, and black velvet cap with gold fringe authorized by the Jockey Club had first been seen at Newmarket in 1877, when the Prince's Arab steed, Alep, had been beaten by thirty lengths by Avowal, another Arab. Undeterred by this initial failure, the Prince had decided to train horses of his own at John Porter's Kingsclere stables. After eight years'

York Cottage, seen from the north-east, with Humbert's original residence for the male guests at Sandringham House on the right.

racing the 1885 season yielded him a mere £296. Two years later, however, Porter acquired Perdita II, the mare that was to lay the foundation for the Prince's later success, though success seemed remote in 1892 when the Prince withdrew from Porter's Hampshire establishment. [13] Then in 1893 the Prince appointed Richard Marsh, who operated from Lordship Farm, Newmarket, as his new trainer. The immediate result was that Florizel II, son of Perdita II, was placed second on one occasion. In 1894

The Prince of Wales's family in 1895. Standing, left to right: Princess Louise, Duchess of Fife; Albert Edward, Prince of Wales; Victoria Mary, Duchess of York; Princess Maud of Wales; Prince Charles of Denmark.
Seated, left to right: Alexander, Duke of Fife; George, Duke of York, holding his son, Prince Edward; Alexandra, Princess of Wales; Princess Victoria of Wales.

1896   Reproduced by gracious permission of Her Majesty the Queen   1898   Reproduced by gracious permission of Her Majesty the Queen

Florizel II won five races netting £3,499 in prize-money and he won six times more in 1895. Florizel's famous full brother, Persimmon won two races in the same year. In 1896 Persimmon achieved greatness taking the Derby, the St Leger, and the Jockey Club Stakes and in 1897 he won the Eclipse Stakes and the Gold Cup. Persimmon went to stud but by 1899 another full brother, Diamond Jubilee, appeared among the winners. In 1900 the fantastic Diamond Jubilee took the Two Thousand Guineas, the Newmarket Stakes, the Derby, the Eclipse Stakes, and the St Leger.

The Princess of Wales, holding the reins, enjoying a drive round the Sandringham estate on a sunny November day in 1896. Standing at the side is the Duchess of York, later Queen Mary. This circular snapshot was probably taken with one of the Kodak cameras that their inventor, George Eastman, presented to members of the Royal Family a few years after he had introduced the first convenient camera for amateurs in 1889. The Princess of Wales, later Queen Alexandra, became a most enthusiastic photographer.[14]

Princess Alexandra, showing her grandson, Prince Edward (later King Edward VIII) around the Sandringham Kennels on the West Newton road in 1898.

Hudson and Kearns 1901   *Country Life*

Persimmon, with Lord Marcus Beresford (right), one of the Prince of Wales's racing advisers.

7
King Edward VII

1901-1910

King Edward VII leaving the main entrance of Sandringham House. In the background is The Joss.

IN 1901 THE PRINCE OF WALES ascended the Throne as King Edward VII only to reign a mere nine years. Inevitably he spent far less time at Sandringham, omitting his summer visits entirely and always leaving the 'Big House' soon after Christmas. However, Queen Alexandra, who retained her charm and gaiety well into her seventies, spent much of her time there without him. Her only surviving son, the Duke of York was, of course, often only five minutes away at York Cottage, and her youngest daughter, soon to be Queen Maud of Norway, was given Appleton House, Mrs Cresswell's former home.

1902   Norfolk County Libraries

King's Lynn celebrating the Coronation of King Edward VII on 9 August 1902.

C.M. Sheldon   Gresham Publishing Company

The distribution of Christmas gifts by the Prince of Wales. In 1866 there were '616 recipients in 169 families. The boys of the Princess' schools had a tweed jacket and blue cap, the girls a scarlet cloak and a hat. At 4 p.m. . . . the Prince and the Duke of Edinburgh [behind the Prince] . . . entered the carriage house, which was dressed with evergreens and had ranges of tables spread with beef. Each man and woman received two pounds, each child one pound, and each widow four pounds.' After 1883 these ceremonies took place in the Sandringham House Ballroom.

Christmas each year meant extensively decorating the Sandringham ballroom with wreaths and garlands. There were some eight hundred gifts to be got ready. So far as the estate staff was concerned, Christmas festivities at Sandringham began on the afternoon of Christmas Eve. The King and his family issued all the outdoor staff with joints of meat (the distribution to the indoor staff was made on New Year's Day). A further distribution of presents followed in the evening. [1]

With the passing years the balls at Sandringham never reached the number held prior to the death of the Duke of Clarence. In 1901 King Edward VII, then Prince of Wales, became as fond of theatricals as his mother the Queen. There survives a list of the presents he gave to Henry Kemble, Arthur Playfair, and others for performances in 1906. [2]

The turn of the century had seen the arrival of a car for the King and the electric light was installed at both Sandringham House and York Cottage. 'We had a splendid motor car down there and I did enjoy being driven about in the cool of the evening at 50 miles an hour', [3] Queen Alexandra wrote of one novelty and of the other: 'The electric light is perfect.' [4] In addition Queen Alexandra had a Columbia electric carriage worked by batteries, just powerful enough to use inside the grounds.

Radio Times Hulton Picture Library

1911

Radio Times Hulton Picture Library

The Royal Tutor, Henry Peter Hansell, a very conscientious though somewhat humourless Norfolkman of towering stature, with Prince Edward (left) and Prince Albert.
Many years later, all four surviving sons of King George V sent wreaths to Hansell's funeral in Norwich Cathedral.

The Duke and Duchess of York's first child was born at White Lodge, Richmond, the Duke's mother's home; he was Prince Edward (1894-1972), later King Edward VIII (right). The Royal couple's other five children were all born at York Cottage, Prince Albert (1895-1952), later King George VI (left) and Princess Mary (1897-1965) later Countess of Harewood (centre), being the eldest of these. This picture was probably taken in 1902 when Edward was seven, Albert six, and Mary approaching five.

E. Bullock *c.* 1869　　　　　　　　　　　　　　Norfolk County Libraries

The main lime tree avenue looking north towards the Norwich Gates.

1903　　　　　　　　　　　　　　*Illustrated London News*

The fire of 10 December 1903, showing the burnt-out rafters of the Honourable Charlotte Knollys's room.

W. Ralph 1913　　　　　　　　　　　　　　The Editor

Sandringham Fire Brigade in 1913. The Brigade was merged with Norfolk County Fire Service in 1968.

In December 1903 another fire broke out at Sandringham, but one that did comparatively little damage. After the fire of 1891 the King had had all the floors strengthened on Messrs Homan and Rogers's patent system. The fire started in the bedroom of the Honourable Charlotte Knollys where a fireplace had recently been installed. It was inadequately insulated from the ceiling of the Queen's room which lay immediately below. No one can blame the august lady-in-waiting for stoking up well although she was horrified to realize that the heat had penetrated the concrete hearthstone to the rafters below. Queen Alexandra lost a good many articles of sentimental value in the blaze. 'Terrible smoke . . . with a crash down came half my ceiling. . . . God saved us. Shock has done no harm to Charlotte. . . . Luckily neither her sitting-room nor my dressing room were touched . . . a good many of my precious souvenirs and things, books and photos, etc. were both burnt or spoilt by fire or water.'[5]

In 1908 there was another great gale which demolished so many trees, including the avenue of limes, that the House became visible from the road.[6] The King had the Norwich Gates moved and the road diverted in an effort to restore a measure of privacy but the problem was not fully solved for another thirty years.

King Edward VII's interest in Sandringham never flagged. The bowling-alley, his delight of forty years earlier, was converted into a library soon after his accession, and he had a nine-hole golf-course laid out. In

Norfolk County Libraries

Right up to his death King Edward VII played a full part in public life. Here he is at the Art Loan Exhibition, King's Lynn on 6 November 1909.

The Author 1976

The meeting point of three architects' work: Humbert's main House is joined to Edis's new turret which is linked (above) to Edis's long extension and (below) to Teulon's conservatory.

Purdy 1928   Norfolk County Libraries

Adrian Jones's statue of Persimmon in front of the Sandringham Stud on the Anmer road, presented by the Jockey Club.

1908 he had Edis open a new entrance on the north, and create yet another turret on the west front with a few extra rooms. The Queen, too, had changes made, mostly in the gardens but her arrangements have long since disappeared. She also had a sumptuous beach-hut made at Snettisham, the nearest point on the coast.

In 1905, Princess Patricia of Connaught, later Lady Patricia Ramsay, a niece of the King and Queen, wrote to her mother, the Duchess of Connaught: 'We motored down to see a little tea house Aunt Alix has built on the beach. I went téte-à-téte with her in her little white motor': this was a Wolseley.[7] At Babingley the Queen set up a small convalescent home for officers wounded in the South African War.[8]

In the Sport of Kings, in the last year of the King's life, his horse Minoru won the Two Thousand Guineas, the Derby, and some less important races. But all in all, taking into consideration both his achievement on the race-course and at stud, Persimmon was undoubtedly the King's most famous and successful horse. He made nearly £127,000 in stud fees before his untimely death in 1908. Of his two brothers, Florizel made close on £93,000 and Diamond Jubilee almost £50,000.[9] There is a fine statue of Persimmon on the Anmer road in front of the Stud.[10] It was presented by the Jockey Club in 1903. The King also indulged in steeplechasing but met with much less success than he had received on the flat.

King Edward VII died at Buckingham Palace on 6 May 1910. Ascending the Throne, his only surviving son George V said of him, 'I have lost my best friend. . . . I never had a word with him in his life.'[11]

WHEN KING GEORGE V referred to Sandringham as 'the place I love better than anywhere else in the world',[1] he was in fact speaking of York Cottage where he had lived for seventeen years, from the time of his marriage. The late King had bequeathed Sandringham House to his widow, Queen Alexandra, and so it was to be another sixteen years before King George and Queen Mary were to occupy the 'Big House'.

Queen Alexandra in her widowhood spent most of her time at Sandringham mainly in the company of her daughter Princess Victoria, Sir Dighton Probyn, who on the death of King Edward VII had become her Comptroller, and Charlotte Knollys. She delighted in calling on her tenants, often with a numerous retinue of her favourite dogs. In the Stables her horses and ponies were a constant delight. She surrounded herself with the many objects of sentimental value which she had gathered over the years. When no longer able to visit her relations in Denmark she enjoyed the companionship of her sister Dagmar (the Empress Marie Feodorovna of Russia) who spent much time with her after the Russian Revolution of 1917. During this period the House was closed to the public although from 1905 the gardens were occasionally opened.

King George V inspecting a Guard of Honour of the Lynn Detachment of the 5th Battalion Norfolk Regiment on his first visit to King's Lynn as monarch on 8 November 1910. Walking before him is his youngest son Prince John then aged five.

8

King George V

1910-1936

1931

Reproduced by gracious permission of Her Majesty the Queen

King George V's Family

King George V
1865-1936

Queen Mary
1867-1953

King Edward VIII
1894-1974

King George VI
1895-1952

Mary
Princess Royal
1897-1956

Henry
Duke of Gloucester
1900-1974

George
Duke of Kent
1902-1942

John
1905-1919

King George V at a shoot at Sandringham with
Queen Mary in 1931.

King George V had been extremely contented at Sandringham before
coming to the Throne. 'After fifteen years in the mysteries of the sea, he
came to learn and love the mysteries of the soil'[2] and references to gardening are frequently found in his meticulously kept diary. The King's enjoyment of Sandringham was cut short in 1914. With the outbreak of the
First World War most of his time was, of necessity, devoted to affairs of
State.

Norfolk County Libraries

The unveiling of the memorial to those of Sandringham who fell in the First World War by King George V, Queen Alexandra, Queen Mary, and Princess Mary in 1920. In 1953 Queen Elizabeth the Queen Mother, unveiled the names of those fallen in the Second World War.

Sandringham itself did not escape the war. It was on 19 January 1915 that Zeppelin L45 crossed the North Sea on the first raid of the war and bombed parts of Norfolk. Several bombs landed on and around the Royal estate. *The Milwaukee Free Press* for January 1915 reported inaccurately, 'Zeppelins bombard Sandringham as King George and the Queen flee.'[3] One of the craters at Wolferton filled with water and became the haunt of ducks. King George VI had it enlarged and it became known as 'Wolferton Splash'.

1915 The Editor

A crater at Snettisham in West Norfolk – a result of the first effective Zeppelin raid on Britain on 19 January 1915.

The ill-fated Gallipoli campaign of 1915 brought tragedy to Sandringham. The Sandringham Brigade, led by Frank Beck, the King's Agent, was trapped in a field, which suddenly burst into flames, possibly due to a stray shell igniting the dry grass. The entire Brigade was annihilated. In 1920 King George V, Queen Alexandra, and Queen Mary unveiled a cross and tablet on the greensward outside Sandringham Church, bearing the names of the fallen.

The King himself suffered an unfortunate wartime accident which had permanent effects on his health and on his comfort when sitting a horse. He was inspecting the newly inaugurated Flying Corps in France on a mare loaned him by Sir Douglas Haig. When the men cheered the mare reared, slipped on the wet ground, and fell backwards on the King, whose courage in minimizing his discomfort was very significant at a time when the War was moving against the Allies.

In 1915 King George spent his usual family Christmas at Sandringham. The following year on 11 January 1916 Queen Mary wrote to her brother: 'weather . . . abominable. George is ever so much better for being in the country and is shooting fairly well though he is a bit lame still. . . . David [the Prince of Wales] is with us which is a great pleasure. . . . Bertie [Prince Albert] is certainly better and beginning to put on weight . . . shooting much less artificial than it used to be . . . G[eorge] has done very little preparing th[is] last year, the birds are few and far between and the colossal bags of former years are no longer so big.'[4]

'King George was easily the best shot of any monarch, live or dead',[5] – this claim was based on the comments of the many experienced and widely travelled shots who had been in the King's company at Balmoral and at Sandringham on many occasions. They recalled that King Edward VII, as Prince of Wales, had been far more concerned with the impeccable arrangements of his shoots, and with the systems which brought the greatest bags, than with his own prowess. He had ensured that his second son had practised shooting with a single-barrelled gun when ten years of age so that it was quite natural that the son, quieter and more concentrated in his manner, was the better shot. In 1935 when King George was seventy, weakened by a war injury and by serious bronchial illness he still retained his skill. King Carlos I of Portugal (1863-1908) was reputed to approach the English King's skill and Kaiser Wilhelm II (1859-1941) was an enthusiastic shot, but the withered arm with which he was afflicted at birth stopped his attaining the first rank. Of subsequent monarchs, King Edward VIII attended Sandringham shooting-parties as Prince of Wales, and occasionally showed considerable skill, but he was never very enthusiastic. There is a well-known story concerning Prince Edward as marksman. The Prince was out shooting with his father, King George V, who ordered him to the end of the line for bad shooting. The Prince obeyed his father and went to the end of the line where he took out a newspaper and began to read. Some time later a bird came over very high which, much to his father's surprise, the Prince killed with his first barrel.

King George V was accompanied on his shoots by his white pony Jock. He took personal charge of all the details of the day's shoot, even to the placing of the guns. He was always careful to avoid disturbing each season's nesting birds. A keen member of the Norfolk and Norwich Naturalists' Trust, he had a white-tailed eagle on the estate protected.

George V was the first monarch to interest himself solely in working dogs, for show, or for following up the beaters when shooting. He used labrador retrievers and clumber spaniels. The great virtue of the spaniels was their ability to penetrate the thick clumps of rhododendrons though

Radio Times Hulton Picture Library

General Sir Dighton Probyn, V.C. (1833-1924), Comptroller and Treasurer to the Prince of Wales (later King Edward VII). In 1910 he became Comptroller to the widowed Queen Alexandra, to whom he was devoted. The summer house, the Nest, which he placed on the west lawn in her honour in 1913, is delightfully tiled and bears the inscription 'Today tomorrow and every day God bless her and guard her I fervently pray'. Queen Alexandra did not long survive her old servant. After he lost his wife in 1900 it was thought he might marry the Hon. Charlotte Knollys, The Queen's lady-in-waiting but he did not, although he did give her for her bathroom 'one mass of mirrors, so that I believe you can see yourself reflected 28 times'.[6] Probyn's own bathroom contained three basins labelled 'Head and face only', 'Hands', and 'Teeth'.[7]

1934   Reproduced by gracious permission of Her Majesty the Queen

George V touring his estate on his favourite pony Jock.

Kingsway   Norfolk County Libraries

During King Edward VII's reign (1901-10) there were over fifty dogs in the Kennels. Queen Alexandra delighted in breeding unusual specimens: rough-haired bassets (dogs of dachshund type), deer hounds, and Borzois (Russian wolfhounds). The Borzoi Vassilka, shown here with the kennelman, took numerous prizes for the King and Queen.

the labradors did the actual retrieving. In his time only the clumber spaniels were housed in the Royal Kennels, the labradors being kept by their keepers. King George V's Wolferton Jet, a labrador bitch, took second place at Cruft's in 1916.

King George V's successes on the racecourse never equalled those of his father. Nevertheless, he was the first reigning monarch to breed and own a classic winner. This was the mare Scuttle, who unfortunately died at the Sandringham Stud while foaling. Scuttle won the Two Thousand Guineas for the King in 1928 and had other successes.

Since he had first moved into York Cottage the King had taken an interest in the Royal pigeons. The flock was founded at Sandringham in 1886. Almost annually several were entered in international contests and when the King visited the Naval Centre at Lowestoft during the First World War he sent off a pigeon carrying a message for Sandringham.[8] Pigeons from the Royal Lofts also saw active service with the Royal Air Force in the Second World War.

Sandringham was to prove a financial liability to more than one monarch. During and after the First World War estate costs rose rapidly and King George V had to contribute towards the expenses of Sandringham House even though he was still living at York Cottage.

Apart from Christmas and the winter shooting-parties, some of the happiest Sandringham occasions for the King were concerned with the

Kingsway   Norfolk County Libraries

The old Stables, now part of the Museum, on the east of Sandringham grounds, early in the century. Horses were seldom put down even during the First World War, when every means of saving expense and manpower was being sought. Queen Alexandra said, 'it breaks my heart that this cruel war should be the cause of my having to consent to let so many of my precious old friends, my horses, be slaughtered after all these years of faithful service. One pony Beau I will not sacrifice.'[9]

1922   Reproduced by gracious permission of Her Majesty the Queen

Queen Alexandra feeding one of the hounds at the meet of the West Norfolk Hunt on 9 January 1922. Behind her are King George V; Queen Mary; and the King's sister Princes Louise, Princess Royal and Duchess of Fife.

Purdy   Norfolk County Libraries

Queen Alexandra retained her beauty until the end of her life. She is seen here at Sandringham Flower Show in July 1922 with her sister-in-law, Queen Olga of the Hellenes.

Bertram Park   Camera Club

The Duchess of York, now Queen Elizabeth the Queen Mother, shortly after her marriage.

marriages of his children. His only daughter, Princess Mary, became engaged to Lord Lascelles at York Cottage in 1921. She was married in 1922 and one of her bridesmaids was Lady Elizabeth Bowes-Lyon (now Queen Elizabeth the Queen Mother) who was to marry the Duke of York in 1923. The King was immediately drawn to her, uncharacteristically saying on one occasion when she and her husband were late for dinner, 'I think we must have sat down two minutes too early.'

In 1925 Queen Alexandra died at the age of eighty-one. Her constant companions of her last years had been her unmarried daughter Princess Victoria and her two faithful retainers of whom Sir Dighton Probyn had died, aged ninety-one, just before his revered Queen and the Hon. Charlotte Knollys who was now nearly ninety. The King arranged for Princess Victoria to move from Sandringham to The Coppins at Iver in Buckinghamshire, and for the Hon. Charlotte Knollys to move into a Grace and Favour home.

Queen Mary must have been pleased to occupy the 'Big House' after the thirty-three years at York Cottage. In 1898 she had written: 'I have less room than ever for all my numerous belongings.'[10] After she moved into Sandringham House in 1926, she wrote to her brother Adolphus, Marquess of Cambridge, 'much has been removed so that one now has the feeling of space and air which was sadly lacking.'[11]

When Queen Mary, for the first time, spent some of the summer of 1926 at Sandringham the King had hoped to join her. Prince Edward had been helping his mother rearrange the old furnishings and pictures. 'I am glad he took an interest in it,' wrote the King from London, 'although he certainly didn't stop long, but rushed off to his tiresome golf.'[12]

The former Royal Home of York Cottage was converted into estate offices and flats and Beach House, Queen Alexandra's summer retreat at Snettisham, was abandoned.

Unfortunately, not long after he had taken over Sandringham House from his deceased mother, King George was to suffer a serious illness (1928-29) which kept him away from his Norfolk country home for well over a year.

At one time the King had hoped to pay regular summer visits to Sandringham, but this proved impossible. He did have a lift installed in Sandringham House but few other changes were made. When in residence the King for the most part enjoyed quiet indoor pursuits: listening to the gramophone; collating his stamps; playing a game of poker. He was the first British monarch to broadcast to the Empire from the so-called 'business-room' at Sandringham. This was on Christmas Day 1932.

It was at Sandringham on 20 January 1938 when the King lay dying that the B.B.C. broadcast to the nation that most poignant bulletin: 'The King's life is moving peacefully towards its close.'

The funeral of Queen Alexandra on 26 November 1925. King George V leads the mourners.

Queen Alexandra's coffin being transferred from the gun-carriage to the train at Wolferton Station on 26 November 1925.

THE DEATH OF KING GEORGE V saw the new King, Edward VIII, at Sandringham – but not for long. He almost immediately flew to London in order to be in the capital for the proclamation of his accession to the Throne. The King's hurried withdrawal from Sandringham however, was symptomatic – he had never been as fond of the estate as his father and brother. Fort Belvedere, the home of his choice, lay in Surrey – a county of mild climate in sharp contrast to Norfolk where the wind on the heath blows mostly from the north-east.

It now seems that King Edward VIII identified Sandringham with the restrictive and repressive régime imposed upon him by his father. It is recognised that King George V had, in dealing with his eldest son, possibly exerted his authority with an unwonted severity.

The accumulated repressions of many years were about to be released and the household at Sandringham was among the first to feel the effects.

A few of the immediate changes were of a minor character but others by implication were far-reaching. For instance, King Edward VIII showed himself to be at one with his grandmother Queen Victoria in objecting to Sandringham time and Greenwich Mean Time became the norm.

However the King called upon his brother, the Duke of York, to investigate the whole administration of the estate with a view to making economies. This development caused consternation and Edmund Beck, the Sandringham Agent, and the third member of his family to hold the post, handed in his resignation and this was accepted.

The changes continued. The King preferred hunting to shooting so the number of game birds was drastically cut down. The breeding of cattle was confined to Wolferton and Appleton and the flax-growing experiment inaugurated by King George V at Flitcham in 1934, having proved uneconomic, was terminated. Finally the number of persons employed directly by the Crown was reduced.

In his brief reign King Edward VIII spent less than one day at Sandringham, and in the ordinary course of events the estate would probably have provided a home for the widowed Queen Mary, as it had in the case of Queen Alexandra. But this was not to be. The Abdication changed everything. To the emotional difficulties of the time were added financial ones. Sandringham, with Balmoral was in the personal possession of King Edward VIII. 'Under the wills of Queen Victoria and King George V, King Edward VIII was a life tenant. Any satisfactory financial settlement had to be based on the transference of the estates to his brother. Informed guesses put the figure for Sandringham and Balmoral at one million pounds and the yearly income paid by George VI to his brother at £60,000.'[1]

Reproduced by gracious permission of Her Majesty the Queen

The Prince of Wales with his sister Princess Mary at Sandringham. He did not frequently visit the estate in adult life although his childhood holidays and schooldays were spent at York Cottage. The Duchess of Windsor, whom he married on 3 June 1937, states: 'The Duke preferred Fort Belvedere, as he had grown to dislike large palaces such as Sandringham, and felt happier in the greater coziness of the Fort, which was lacking in pretension and pomp.'

9

King Edward VIII

1936

1937

Colin Osman

10 King George VI

1936-1952

King George VI, Queen Elizabeth, Princess Elizabeth, and Princess Margaret, with Keeper, J. Walter Jones, at the Royal Pigeon Lofts, Sandringham, in 1937. The Duke of York started a loft of racing pigeons in 1893. The Royal Pigeon Lofts have now been moved from Sandringham to Gaywood, King's Lynn.

KING GEORGE VI enjoyed life at Sandringham as much as had his father before him. Within a fortnight of his unexpected succession to the Throne and the departure of his brother, the King and his immediate family spent Christmas at Sandringham, a tradition which continued until the outbreak of the Second World War.

The upheaval caused by the war affected the King much as it affected many of his subjects. At Sandringham the nine-hole golf course was put under the plough and it was decided to close down the 'Big House'. Nevertheless, it was from Sandringham House that the King commenced broadcasting his Christmas messages to the Empire. Because of a speech impediment it was an act of courage for the King to broadcast at all but in the first broadcast of Christmas 1939 he came through with flying colours. In his broadcast he made apt use of a quotation from Miss M. L. Haskins: 'I said to the man who stood at the gate of the Year "Give me a light that I may tread safely into the unknown." And he replied: "Go out into the darkness and put your hand into the Hand of God. That shall be to you better than light and safer than a known way." '

Marcus Adams 1936

One of the peacetime activities carried on by the King during the war was in the field of racing where in 1944 he headed the list of winning owners.

With the return of peace life at Sandringham was resumed, as were the traditional family Christmases. The family were glad to be back in the Big House for Christmas, 'to know that the telephone or telegrams would no longer bring tragic news of friends or relatives, to pay no attention to the friendly aircraft roaring overhead from the nearby American bases, to pay no heed to the soft drone of bombers in the night . . . Sandringham, as every home in Britain, celebrated the inimitable zest of the first post-war Christmas.'[1]

King George VI's mode of shooting differed both from those of King Edward VII and King George V, being much more informal and tending to take the bird on the wing rather than when driven by beaters. The future King George VI's first shooting experience was the capture of three rabbits at Wolferton Warren on 23 December 1907, when he was twelve. 'It was . . . the beginning of an era. During the decades which followed the whole pattern of shooting was to become subject to radical change and the rigid formality of the pre-arranged shoot was to disappear. Two or even

Queen Elizabeth with Princess Elizabeth and Princess Margaret.

Reproduced by gracious permission of Her Majesty the Queen

Queen Mary next to her only daughter, the Princess Royal (1897-1965) at a bazaar at Sandringham Rectory in August 1951. In the dark coat is the Queen's lady-in-waiting, Lady Cynthia Colville.

1948

Reproduced by gracious permission of Her Majesty the Queen

A snapshot of four generations of the Royal Family taken at Sandringham in 1948. Back row (left to right) the Duke of Gloucester, Queen Elizabeth, Queen Mary, King George VI, Prince Philip and Princess Marina. Front row (left to right) the Duke of Kent, Prince William and Prince Richard of Gloucester, Princess Alexandra and Prince Michael of Kent, Princess Elizabeth and Princess Margaret.

three sets of beaters were to give place in time to perhaps half a dozen men, and hand reared birds after the Second World War were to become an exception.'[2] Although King George VI's shooting was never on the scale of his father's, it was much more diverse. The King did not like shooting in large groups and one of the pre-war entries in his Game Diary states: 'snow and very cold east wind. I spent four hours in a hide in a kale field.'

The King's Game Book was impeccably kept. He took a particular interest in his woodcock records, making up his own total separately in red ink from the first one he ever shot at Sandringham on 17 December 1911. Only twice in Norfolk did his score of woodcock attain double figures, but he shot 1,055 during his career, 928 in Norfolk.

In the field King George VI had the good manners of his grandfather, King Edward VII, and would walk with the beaters. Characteristically, his Game Book, covering forty-five years, includes neither praise of his own shooting nor criticism of anyone else's. Flighting, as duck-shooting is called, appealed to King George VI because it consisted in intercepting a bird on its natural round, whereas with game-shooting, birds were shot which, if left to their natural devices, would not be on the wing.

Wildfowling certainly demands more skill than pheasant- or partridge-shooting which is so dependent on the efforts of the beaters. King George VI also enjoyed the coot shoot on Hickling Broad with which the Norfolk season traditionally ended. There is in the gun-room at Sandringham House a small, single-barrelled, muzzle-loading gun from which King Edward VII, the Duke of Clarence, King George V, King Edward VIII, and King George VI all fired their first shots.

King George VI also had a great influence in the design of the gardens at Sandringham. G. A. Jellicoe who designed the North Gardens recalls: 'King George knew precisely what he wanted in landscape. Though he was not always familiar with the technique of getting it, he was able to detect if the experts were moving on the wrong lines. Many of his instructions were accompanied by his own pencil notes, and these provided a basis of discussion on which the design would develop. He would pass constantly from drawings to the site and back again . . . and he took a hand in all setting out by the contractor, enjoying as much as anyone the rough and tumble of earth works.' The King had a particular fondness for woodland and spent much time in improving the Glade.[3]

Life inside the 'Big House' assumed a greater informality – for instance, decorations were no longer worn at dinner. Christmas 1946 was made significant by the appearance of Prince Philip of Greece for the first time at the family party.

King George VI had all his life suffered frequently from bouts of ill health and on 6 February 1952 he died at the Sandringham he loved so much. Only in the previous year he had written to his mother from Sandringham: 'I have always been so happy here and I love the place.'

1948   J. L. Chalcraft

King George VI with Princess Margaret at the opening of the Wolferton pumping station on 2 February 1948. The King had given the land on which the pumping station was built.

1951

Reproduced by gracious permission of Her Majesty the Queen

King George VI and Queen Mary with their grandchildren Prince Charles and Princess Anne at Sandringham for the Christmas of 1951. Two months later King George was dead and Princess Elizabeth became Queen.

1943   Hutchinson

Princess Elizabeth during the gathering of the Sandringham wartime harvest of 1943.

PRINCESS ELIZABETH'S FIRST VISIT to Sandringham took place at Christmas 1926 when she was just eight months old. It was a short visit. Having been embraced by 'Grandpapa England' (King George V) and Queen Mary and admired by the guests at the 'Big House', she returned with her parents, the Duke and Duchess of York, to their home at St Paul's Waldenbury. From that time the Princess made frequent visits to Sandringham and in 1930 was accompanied for the first time by her sister, Princess Margaret Rose. The Princesses lived quietly and privately, their parents shielding them from premature exposure to the public gaze. Stories and pictures of the Princesses appeared regularly in the Press but always a certain reticence was maintained.

On 20 December 1936 the life of Princess Elizabeth was changed dramatically for on that day her father succeeded to the Throne as King George VI. As heir to the Throne her privacy became increasingly difficult to maintain until with the outbreak of war in 1939 more sombre events filled the headlines.

During the Second World War the Princesses were frequently resident on the Sandringham estate. They lived at Appleton House which had been specially strengthened against bomb attacks. Here they enjoyed the usual country pursuits and in 1943 Princess Elizabeth was featured in the Press helping with the harvest.

11

Queen Elizabeth II

1952 to the present day

Jarrolds   Reproduced by gracious permission of Her Majesty the Queen

Her Majesty the Queen on Cossack.

1952   Pitkin Pictorials

The Times 1934   Reproduced by gracious permission of
Her Majesty the Queen

Two monarchs broadcasting from the business-room at Sandringham House. Queen Elizabeth II's first Christmas broadcast of 1952 and King George V, who was the first monarch to broadcast to the nation, making his Christmas broadcast of 1934.

RIGHT: The Great Saloon.
Jarrolds 1977   Reproduced by gracious permission of
Her Majesty the Queen

At the end of the war in 1945 the 'Big House' was reopened and Princess Elizabeth rejoiced with her family at once more taking up residence. Prince Philip of Greece attended Princess Elizabeth for the first time at Sandringham during the Christmas of 1946. Prince Philip did a good deal of shooting at Sandringham and was personally instructed in the art of wildfowling by King George VI. The following year on 20 November 1947 the young couple were married in Westminster Abbey. Their first-born son, Prince Charles, was only five weeks old when he spent his first Christmas at Sandringham in 1948.

In February 1952 Princess Elizabeth accompanied by her husband, now the Duke of Edinburgh, left England to tour Africa. After bidding them farewell at the airport King George VI and Queen Elizabeth returned to Sandringham House. Here, quite suddenly, on the night of 6 February 1952 King George VI died of a heart attack. Princess Elizabeth received the tragic news of her father's death in Kenya and in less than twenty-four hours was back in England to assume her responsibilities being hailed as Queen by the Prime Minister, Winston Churchill.

That same Christmas, Queen Elizabeth was host at Sandringham for the first time and also made her first Christmas broadcast from the same small business-room used by her father and her grandfather before her.

Eastern Counties Newspapers

Queen Elizabeth II with her youngest child,
Prince Edward, on her knee; Prince Andrew;
and Queen Elizabeth the Queen Mother, leaving
Wolferton Station for their stay at Sandringham
in December 1964.

1954   Eastern Counties Newspapers

The Queen Mother was made a Freeman of the
Borough of King's Lynn on 28 July 1954.
Replying to the Mayor, Bernard Bremner, she
said: 'King's Lynn, lying as it does so close to my
home where I have spent so many happy days,
has long held a special place in my heart . . . there
is one duty Mr Mayor, amongst those which you
mentioned which will certainly never trouble
me – to defend the town against the Sovereign's
enemies – for I well know that in this county
there are none.'

Later, when television became popular Her Majesty made the first two
Christmas appearances – those of 1957 and 1958 – in the Library at
Sandringham. Because of the large number of technical staff and the
masses of equipment needed for television all subsequent Christmas
messages have been pre-recorded at Buckingham Palace.

The Queen and the Duke of Edinburgh take a great interest in the
running of the Sandringham estate. Many changes have been made and
there has been a marked improvement in productivity. A bacon piggery
holding 2,000 beasts has been installed and an apple-packing station
erected. Corn, sugar-beet, potatoes, onions, and mustard are successfully
grown and areas given over to the production of peas and carrots have
been introduced. In common with a number of other Norfolk farmers, the
Queen invites the public to come to the Royal fruit farms to 'Pick your
own Worcester apples'. The Reverend Patrick Ashton formerly Vicar of
Sandringham writes: 'The home farms, consisting of some 3,000 acres, are
mixed arable and beef farming . . . cattle are sent to agricultural shows all
over Britain and win many prizes. About 2,000 acres of woodland are
being extensively reafforested . . . all the parkland is grazed with cattle and
the produce from the gardens is sent to Buckingham Palace and for sale to
various markets. The remaining 15,000 acres of the estate are let to tenant
farmers.'

The Queen and the Duke of Edinburgh spend as much time at
Sandringham as their public duties will allow. They no longer arrive by

Hutchinson

Queen Elizabeth II, Queen Elizabeth the Queen Mother (left), and Prince Charles (on the pony, right), at a meet of the West Norfolk Hunt. The Queen's aunt, the Princess Royal, is on Her Majesty's left.

Reproduced by gracious permission of Her Majesty the Queen

Queen Elizabeth II, the Duke of Edinburgh, and Prince Edward at the Royal Kennels in 1973.

rail. The sumptuous Royal waiting-rooms at Wolferton Station were used for the last time for shooting luncheons in 1967. Later the whole complex was put up for public auction. Nowadays the Royal Family arrive by road or by air.

A good deal of the Queen's leisure time is occupied with horses. Her Majesty is an accomplished horsewoman, as is, of course, her daughter, Princess Anne. In 1954 the Queen was the leading owner, taking £35,799 in prize-money. Many of Her Majesty's horses have retired to Sandringham, among them the Queen Mother's Devon Loch which just failed to win the Grand National in 1956 and the Queen's famous horse, Aureole, which died on the estate in 1974.

In 1975 Sandringham House underwent a major change when ninety-one rooms were demolished in an effort to ease the problem of running a large establishment with the much smaller staff of today. The work – the largest undertaken since the fire of 1891 – was skilfully executed and suprisingly is hardly noticeable. At the same time repairs were made to the lead of the roof and to some of the stonework. The House has also been completely rewired and the central heating system improved. It was not until the New Year of 1977 that the Royal Family returned to the 'Big House' although Royal visits to the estate continued, making use of Wood

1974   Eastern Counties Newspapers

The demolition of part of the domestic quarters of Sandringham House in 1974. The roofs and some of the stonework of the 'Big House' were also renovated.

Edward Hughes's portrait of Princess Alexandra painted in 1896. The portrait hangs in the Main Drawing Room.

Jarrolds   Reproduced by gracious permission of
                                        Her Majesty the Queen

Eastern Counties Newspapers

During their New Year stay in Norfolk the Queen and the Queen Mother, regularly attend a meeting of the Sandringham Branch of the Women's Institute of which the Queen Mother is President. The Queen is seen here arriving at a meeting in February 1965.

OPPOSITE PAGE:
The Main Drawing Room

Jarrolds   Reproduced by gracious permission of
                                        Her Majesty the Queen

82

1974   Eastern Counties Newspapers

1974   Eastern Counties Newspapers

Farm, an eight-bedroomed house on the Royal estate at Wolferton. The Queen and the Duke of Edinburgh still make informal visits to Wood Farm throughout the year when the main House is open to the public.

In the Jubilee Year of 1977 it was the wish of Her Majesty the Queen that Sandringham House should be opened to the public and the main ground-floor rooms were opened including the Saloon, the Main Drawing Room, the Smaller Drawing Room, the Long Corridor, and the Dining Room. Many family portraits of the nineteenth century adorn the walls, the most notable being Edward Hughes's striking portrait of Princess Alexandra painted in 1896.

Her Majesty encourages people to visit her country home and Sandringham now offers many facilities to the visitor of which the most popular recent innovation is the Museum. Among the exhibits are big game trophies, and cars formerly used by members of the Royal Family together with a Merryweather fire-engine and items of interest concerning the Sandringham Fire Brigade. The Horse Museum includes the head of Persimmon and many photographs and miscellaneous objects relating to the Royal Family's interest in the turf. In 1978 a selection of the Silver Jubilee gifts presented to Her Majesty the Queen was placed on show. The exhibits are regularly changed. The Museum, which was first opened in 1973, is housed in buildings which were formerly the Coach Houses, the Fire Station, Queen Mary's Carving School, and the Power House. Other facilities provided for a growing public include a large car park, a refreshment area, a souvenir shop, a nature trail and picnic area as well as the beautiful grounds and Sandringham House itself, which was so very dear to the hearts of three English Kings.

Queen Elizabeth II visiting the Sandringham Show for the first time in July 1974. The *Eastern Daily Press* reported 'History was made at Sandringham yesterday when five members of the Royal Family, including the reigning sovereign, attended the Show.'

The Duchess of Kent, cousin of the Queen, attending the 1974 Sandringham Show, accompanied by two of her children, the Earl of St Andrews and Lady Helen Windsor.

1965   Eastern Counties Newspapers

Princess Margaret leaving King's Lynn Station with Lord Linley in January 1965 after the Christmas holidays.

12 The Gardens

WHEN THE PRINCE OF WALES acquired Sandringham Hall in 1862 it was fronted by an extensive lake. In 1870 after the rebuilding the Prince of Wales decided to move the lake, which stood too close to the House. The landscape gardener W. B. Thomas was commissioned to execute the work. He excavated two lakes farther south. The two lakes he dotted with small islands. The larger of the lakes afforded an attractive outlook from the Bachelor's Cottage. During the excavations there occurred an incident illustrating the kind-heartedness of Princess Alexandra and at the same time the devotion she invariably evoked. When Thomas broke his leg in the course of his work the Princess showed him such kindness that he sent her white roses on her birthday for the rest of his life.

In front of the House Thomas also created formal gardens after the fashion of Versailles and at one time there was also a Rosary and, near to the Bachelors' Cottage, a maze. Because of the economies dictated by the Second World War and the new informality in garden design these features have now been replaced by lawns. Formerly, the grounds also contained a bear-pit – for Charlie and his mate Polly – a monkey-house, and an aviary, as well as other enclosures specifically designed for the preservation of the many animals presented to

Hudson and Kearns 1901   *Country Life*
The Rosary and its ornamental fountain in 1901.

the Prince of Wales or brought home from his foreign travels.

Fifty and more years ago interest in the West Gardens centred not only in the formal beds but also in the Dell described by W. A. Dutt as containing: 'charming nooks where, in a shade as of a cloister, the ferns dip the tips of their fronds in the clear water.'

F. Ralph 1863   Norfolk County Libraries
Sandringham Hall in 1863, showing the proximity of the lake to the Hall.

Norfolk County Libraries
The west front of Sandringham House showing the lake replaced by ornamental gardens.

LEFT:
The west front of Sandringham House
Jarrolds   Reproduced by gracious permission of
Her Majesty the Queen

One of the earliest ornaments to be placed in the grounds has always been known as 'The Joss'. The word *joss*

F. Frith 1891   Norfolk County Libraries
The Joss

means idol, and the statue, dating from 1690, is of gold plate on bronze, and represents the Buddhist divinity Kuvera. It was brought back from Peking in the battleship H.M.S. *Rodney* by Sir Henry Keppel (1809-1904) who came to be known as 'The Father of the Navy'. The statue was shipped to King's Lynn and finished its journey by road, arriving at Sandringham in 1870. The Prince of Wales was delighted with the gift and a pagoda-style wooden canopy was constructed for it – this has since been removed.

Princess Alexandra had a dairy built by the Anmer road near the Stables. It was influenced in design by the Swiss Cottage standing in the grounds of Osborne House, Queen Victoria's

RIGHT:
Sandringham from the air. In the foreground is the Church of St Mary Magdalene. To the left of the House the North Gardens, beyond the East Gardens and Persimmon greenhouses. Among the trees can be seen the Museum complex. York Cottage is off the picture to the right.

Reproduced by gracious permission of
Her Majesty the Queen

retreat on the Isle of Wight. A contemporary account relates: 'It is really a Swiss cottage, and served not only for a dairy but also as a rendezvous for afternoon tea. The portion devoted to business is covered with tiles, which were a present from the King [Edward VII], having been selected and ordered for the purpose by His Majesty when in Bombay some years earlier. . . . This dairy has not been so much in use lately as it formerly was, but at one time the Princess and her daughters were frequently to be found busily engaged in turning out tempting looking pats of butter, themselves clad in apron and sleeves in true business-like style.' The dairy was popular and was visited by many notable guests including Queen Victoria who presented a tea-service decorated with hand-painted views of Balmoral.

Most of the work undertaken in the gardens was initiated in the Prince of Wales's time. Quite early on Pulham, one of the gardeners, constructed the Rock Garden above the upper lake and the Boathouse and Grotto, built in a massive style from blocks of carstone.

Hudson and Kearns 1901   *Country Life*   Hudson and Kearns 1901   *Country Life*

Princess Alexandra's Dairy – the exterior and the interior.

The Flower and Vegetable Gardens, however, were established on the eastern side of the Hillington Road in 1905. Their most striking feature is a pergola some seventy yards in length – the longest in England. The brick piers are fifteen feet high and support cross-timbers fashioned from trees grown on the estate. Behind this area are the teak greenhouses named after King Edward VII's famous racehorse Persimmon. These are used for the culture of tomatoes, melons, roses, orchids, carnations and chrysanthemums – as well as all the general pot plants and cut flowers required for the House.

In 1906 there were ninety-one gardeners at work in the grounds, now there are only twelve. Nowadays, of course, much use is made of machinery and of the new insecticides.

After the great gale of 1908 when many of the lime trees flanking the main drive were uprooted and the remainder had to be cut down, King Edward VII had the boundary wall set back a farther 160 yards from the House, enclosing part of Dersingham Wood. The public road was diverted

and the Glade planted in its place. None the less at certain times of the year the House remained visible from the road.

The year 1908 saw the gardens opened to the public for the first time. The proceeds from the admission charges have always gone to named charities. The list of these charities is extensive and is reviewed annually. Produce from the gardens is given to local hospitals.

After King Edward VII's death in 1910 Sir Dighton Probyn became Comptroller to Queen Alexandra, to whom he was devoted. He called her 'The Blessed Lady' and presented her in 1913 with a pretty summer house, close to the lake, called 'the Nest'. Inside the inscription reads:

The Queen's Nest – A small offering to The Blessed Lady from Her Beloved Majesty's very devoted old servant General Probyn 1913 – Today tomorrow and every day God bless her and guard her I fervently pray.

King George VI had his rooms at the northern end of Sandringham House and it was he who ultimately solved the problem of the lack of privacy from

F. Ralph 1911   Norfolk County Libraries

The Pergola

the road by creating a raised shrubbery bed and diverting the drive round it.

The King also created the North Gardens. They were designed by G. A. Jellicoe, and consist of a series of formal arrangements bordered by box hedges between a double row of lime trees, extending as far as The Joss. The gardens were not complete when work ceased in 1949 but they gave a pleasing aspect from the northern windows and also enabled the King and Queen to reach the Glade in privacy. This was an area favoured by the King and the countless specimens of azaleas and rhododendrons he planted are much in evidence today. In 1950 Queen Mary purchased the statue of Father Time which marks with The Joss the farthest corners of the North Gardens.

One of the oak trees which stands near York Cottage by the lake is over 850 years old, and dates back to the earliest occupation of the estate in Norman times. Extensive planting of both coniferous and deciduous trees has continued since the Henleys' time in the mid eighteenth century. The Royal Family have often marked anniversaries and notable occasions with the planting of trees, particularly oaks. The largest of several oaks in the centre of the lawn facing the main entrance was planted by Queen Victoria during her only formal visit of 1889. In her Diary on 25 April is recorded: 'Out with Bertie [the Prince of Wales] and Alix [The Princess of Wales], Louise [their eldest daughter] and all the children, and I planted a tree in front of the house.' Several

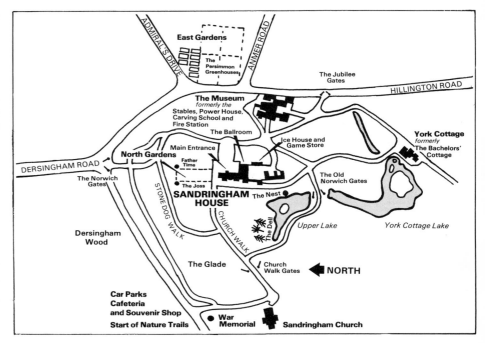

other oaks in front of the house were planted at various times by Queen Alexandra. Queen Mary planted an oak here on her eightieth birthday, on 26 May 1947. Close to where the path between the lakes joins Church Walk is a deodar cedar (Eastern variety) planted by King George V on 11 January 1936, nine days before his death. The seed was at least fifty-four years old. The King recorded in his Diary: 'I planted a cedar in front of the house. Evan-Thomas* brought the seed home in 1882, when he was with us. It was only found after he died four years ago.'

Near to the deodar are two oaks planted by King George VI and Queen Elizabeth in 1937 – the year of the King's Coronation. The tradition has continued to the present day – on 29 April 1977 Her Majesty the Queen planted an oak to commemorate her Silver Jubilee.

There are several gates within the grounds, the oldest of which are the Old Norwich Gates. These were replaced in 1863 by the present Norwich Gates – the wedding present of the County of Norfolk and the City of Norwich to the Prince and Princess of

* Admiral Sir Hugh Evan-Thomas was Senior Naval Cadet when Prince George went to the Royal Naval College at Dartmouth in 1877. Later when Prince George and his elder brother Prince Albert Victor, Duke of Clarence, made a world tour in H.M.S. *Bacchante* in 1882, Evan-Thomas was Senior Midshipman in the gun-room. He later commanded the Fifth Battle Squadron at the Battle of Jutland.

The West Gardens. In the foreground can be seen the entrance to the carstone Boathouse

Wales. The Old Norwich Gates were made in 1724 and date back to the time of the Hoste family and are now situated between the upper and lower lakes. In 1905 the Duke and Duchess of York (later King George V and Queen Mary) presented King Edward VII with a fine pair of wrought-iron gates to form an entrance to the Flower and Vegetable Gardens. The wrought-iron gates which head Church Walk close to Sandringham Church were installed by King Edward VII in 1909 and the magnificent Jubilee Gates on the Hillingdon Road commemorate the Silver Jubilee of King George V in 1935.

The most ambitious scheme for improving the grounds for many years commenced in 1969 when Mr Bodfan Grufydd the landscape-architect was called upon to submit plans to further enhance Sandringham and develop facilities for the visiting public.

The area in front of York Cottage was opened up and a grant of £5,000 received from the Ministry of Housing and Local Government to develop a country park, a scenic drive, and a nature trail.

Jarrolds

Captain Mark Phillips, Princess Anne, H. M. Queen Elizabeth the Queen Mother, H. M. the Queen, Prince Charles, Prince Edward, the Duke of Edinburgh and Lady Sarah Armstrong-Jones.

13

The Royal Parishes

No part of Norfolk can compare, for variety of scenery, with the north-west. The Prince Consort had vision when he selected this area for the Prince of Wales's country home, but he could not have foreseen the century of diligence and devotion by successive Royal owners that was to follow. While never attempting to rival Holkham or Houghton, or even Gunton or Melton Constable, King Edward VII, King George V, King George VI, and Queen Elizabeth II have brought the Sandringham estate to a level of efficiency and attraction never previously approached.

The Royal estate now totals 20,000 acres, compared with the 7,000 or so purchased by the Prince of Wales in 1862. Some of this new land has been reclaimed from the Wash. There are thirteen parishes covered by the Royal estate though not all of them in their entirety.

Anmer

St Mary's Church, Anmer, like many parish churches associated with Norfolk's stately homes, stands in its surrounding park, scarcely a mile to the west of the Roman track, Peddars Way, which joins with the prehistoric Icknield

Anmer Church

Way, near Holme-next-the-Sea, on the northern coast. The older tombs, in the mainly Perpendicular church, are of the Coldham family, at one time Lords of the Manor, but King Edward VII's influence is seen in the reseating of the nave which he paid for in conjunction with a former occupant of Anmer Hall, Vice-Admiral Sir T. F. Hamilton. An unusual feature is the inclusion of three paintings by Sir Noel Paton (1821-1901), one of the most fashionable of Scottish painters of his time.

Anmer Hall

Anmer Hall is a handsome, unusually lengthy, house of typical West Norfolk appearance with brick and carstone intermingled, and a semi-circular porch. It is now the country home of the Queen's cousin, the Duke of Kent and his family. It has six bedrooms, is of two storeys, and has a thirteen-bay frontage; the surrounding parkland comprises some 300 acres.

One of Anmer's most unfortunate inhabitants was Sir Henry Walpole, who lived for a time with his father Christopher in the village from 1578. In 1594 he was put on the rack no less than fourteen times for his Catholicism. He was

hanged, drawn, and quartered on 5 April 1595 and was canonized at the Vatican on 25 October 1970[1] becoming St Henry Walpole.

Anmer has a village sign presented to Queen Elizabeth II by the Norfolk Boy Scouts' Association in 1957, shortly after holding a jamboree on her land. King Edward VII provided a water-supply and a chapel in the village, and there is one of his famous club houses, prominently dated 1909.

Appleton Church

Appleton

The Church of Appleton St Mary, two miles south-east of Sandringham, is in ruins. The nave is fourteenth century. The Paston connection with Appleton is evidenced by a tomb to Agnes Paston in the ruins. Appleton House, rebuilt in 1863 for the Prince's troublesome tenant Louisa Cresswell, became the country home of Queen Maud of Norway (1869-1938), sister of King George V. It has not been tenanted since her death and is unlikely to be again as it was converted into an air-raid shelter for the Royal Family and the Household during the Second World War.

Appleton House

Appleton water-tower

Visually the most interesting building in the vicinity of Appleton is the water-tower by Folkes, built by Prince Albert Edward in 1877. In near-by Denbeck Woods is the site of a Roman villa, excavated in 1947-48, objects from which are displayed in the Sandringham Museum.

Babingley

Babingley Church is another ruin, three miles to the south-west of Sandringham. Standing near the river of the same name, it is one of the holiest sites in East Anglia. St Felix, to whom the church is dedicated, is reputed to have landed here in AD 600, and brought Christianity to eastern England. The event is commemorated in the name of the near-by Christian Hills. The parish used the churchyard for burials until the early twentieth century, but most of the stones are about a century earlier. The church was in ruins when Prince Albert Edward first set foot on his new estate in 1862. The Prince built a corrugated-iron church a good mile away on the main Lynn-Hunstanton road. The Hall is a picturesque moated building now called 'Hall Farm', not far from the ruined church, with stepped gables and a peculiar porch. Built in 1610 it was refronted in carstone by Henry Hoste Henley about 1820,[2] and completely gutted and reorganized after his death for the use of William Durrant, a tenant farmer.[3]

The Three Birchams

Bircham, which is to the north-east of Anmer, just east of the Peddars' Way, has three churches. St Andrew's of Bircham Tofts is ruinous; the other two, both dedicated to St Mary, at Great Bircham and Bircham Newton, have square towers and contain Early English work. Both these churches have box-pews. Great Bircham has an impressive altar-table, and Bircham Newton an early priest's effigy.

The Commonwealth War Graves Cemetery at
Great Bircham.

The War Memorial at Great Bircham singles
out King George VI to head its own parochial list
of dead; His Majesty was, of course, a
serviceman on the estate who died prematurely,
albeit in 1952. The Commonwealth War Graves
Commission cemetery in the churchyard contains
the first Cross of Sacrifice to be set up in Britain
after the Second World War. The churchyard
was originally used for the burial of airmen from
R.A.F. Bircham Newton killed in the Battle of
Britain; eleven German airmen lost in that action
were also buried there. The cemetery now
contains one grave from the First World War
and sixty-seven from the Second. The Cross of
Sacrifice was unveiled by King George VI on 14
July 1946, in the presence of Queen Elizabeth
and the Princesses Elizabeth and Margaret. King
George VI gave an ironwork gate from Queen
Alexandra's rose garden at Sandringham. The
former R.A.F. Station has been converted by the
Construction Industry Training Board Centre
into one of the largest training centres in the
country.

Dersingham Church

Dersingham

Dersingham is one of the most extensive villages
in the district, though it is not all on the Royal
estate. St Nicholas's Church has an impressive
wide nave and tower arch. The Royal Family do
not regularly worship here. A fine church chest,
a painted screen, and a monument to John Pell,
Mayor of Lynn, are some of the interesting
features. In King Edward VII's time Dersingham
Hall, now derelict, was occupied by Mr T.
Jannoch, a pioneer in mass flower production
when refrigeration was in its infancy. The
attractive tithe barn of red brick and carstone,
dated 1671, was recently presented by Queen
Elizabeth II to Norfolk County Council and is in
use as a capacious store for heavy items removed
from old Norfolk buildings which are capable of
re-use. King Edward VII donated the site for a
new Foresters' Hall for which the Prince of
Wales, later George V, laid the foundation-stone.
It was near Dersingham that the last pair of
Great Bustards bred before the huge bird became
extinct in Britain in 1838.

Flitcham Church

Flitcham

Although St Felix is reputed to have built the
first church at Flitcham, its dedication is to St
Mary. Its most interesting features are the three
blank arcading arches each side of the central
tower of Norman date, in carstone. The village
stands on the edge of the park of the now
demolished Hillington Hall and is one of the
smaller villages on the estate, being little more
than a single street. To the east of the village is
the Augustinian Priory of Flitcham, a daughter
house of Walsingham Priory, founded in 1217,
but only a few stones remain today.

Flitcham Village c. 1870

Fring

Fring All Saints is on the northern side of the
estate some four miles south-west of Docking.
The church's most noteworthy feature is a faded
wall-painting of St Christopher dating from
1330. At the White House there are tablets to the

Fring Church

Dusgate family, long Lords of the Manor, who
like so many country gentry sacrificed a son in
the First World War, Richard Edmund Dusgate.
The handsome early nineteenth-century White
House is no longer occupied by the Dusgates.
Distillation of Norfolk lavender is an unusual
but profitable industry carried on in the barn
here.

Sandringham

Sandringham Church is considered the finest
carstone building in existence. Discreetly

Sandringham Church in 1863.

restored by Lady Harriet Cowper in 1885 it contains a very large number of monuments and innumerable items of furniture in precious metals. Rodman Wanamaker II of Philadelphia demonstrated his tremendous admiration for King Edward VII by presenting a silver-faced pulpit and altar as a tribute to his widow Queen Alexandra, who worshipped there so often and with such sincerity.

Wanamaker's silver pulpit has for centrepiece a striking lengthy figure of Christ with the Evangelists, and relief scenes from His ministry. It was presented to Queen Alexandra in 1925, the year of her death. He also presented the silver altar and reredos in 1911, and in 1915 he gave the famous jewelled Bible. The fine Communion Plate he presented in 1927 is kept in Sandringham House. Wanamaker also gave a very heavy processional Spanish cross. The church's glass is mostly nineteenth century, apart from a few seventeenth-century pieces, of which

The statuette of St George.

the most interesting is a depiction of St Frances, who founded an Order known as 'the Collatines' in the fourteenth century. There is no other representation of this Saint in England.

Early monuments date back to the Cobbe occupation of 1517 to 1685, but there is also a series of carved medallions to King Edward VII's mother, brothers, and sisters, and tablets to King George VI and Queen Mary. The monuments to the youngest sons of King Edward VII and King George V, one living for a day and the other for thirteen years, are in the churchyard near the font brought back from Rhodes by King Edward VII's favourite brother, Prince Alfred. The

transept and private vestry on the south side were added for the Royal Family and their suite and the Royal pews contain affectionate inscriptions to lost ones. The west window is a memorial to the Duke of Clarence presented by his brother officers of the 10th Hussars. The famous statuette of St George in aluminium and ivory by Sir Alfred Gilbert is another memorial to the Duke of Clarence. Sir Dighton Probyn, the Prince of Wales's Comptroller, had considerable difficulty in obtaining the commissioned statue from Gilbert. He first complained in January 1889. In September 1901 he wrote: 'I hate doubting anyone's word, but do you wish me to believe *a dozen times* that they [the bas-reliefs] have been completed and *a dozen times* come to grief?' Threats that another sculptor would have to finish the work finally prompted Gilbert to action and the statue was placed at the west end of the Royal pew in 1902.[4]

Louisa Cresswell recalled that the Reverend W.L. Onslow (1866-77) worshipped the Princess 'with an old world reverence and pronounced her name in the service as if it were something between heaven and earth and almost too sacred for mortal voice to utter. The Prince looked rather bored at the services and glad when they were over, which is better than being hypocritical and singing the psalms in a loud voice and appearing to be very devout when you are not.'[5]

Shernborne Church

Shernborne

Shernborne, five miles north-east of Sandringham, has a church with several unusual features. Dedicated to St Peter and St Paul it was rebuilt by the Norwich architect, H. J. Green, in association with Sir Arthur Blomfield at the Prince of Wales's expense. It contains a plaque set by the Princess of Wales (later Queen

Sandringham Church in 1896 and 1960 showing the effect of the embellishments, particularly those of Rodman Wanamaker

Alexandra) 'in gratitude . . . for the merciful preservation of His Royal Highness in Brussels, April 4, 1900', a reference to an incident when the Prince was shot at by a youth named Sipido, at the Gare du Nord – he sustained no injury.

The striking font is described by Pevsner as 'a barbaric but mighty Norman piece'. Shernborne Hall has been partly demolished. There is a licensed club and an adjoining village hall.

West Newton

Although known as the 'King Edward VII's own village', West Newton is probably of more ancient origin than Sandringham. It is on the site of the disappeared Hitchamburg and bears very many signs of King Edward VII and Queen Alexandra's influence. The Alexandra Cottages, a row of substantially built semi-detached dwellings, were erected for the accommodation of the labourers and other employees on the estate in 1864. Later came the Louise Cottages (1870), named after Princess Louise, eldest daughter of King Edward VII and Queen Alexandra; the Mary Cottages for widows and old age pensioners (1925), and Elizabeth Cottages (1937), also for elderly couples. The Victory Cottages (about 1949) brought the total number of model cottages built on the estate to 11,949.

The reputation of the Royal estate housing, particularly that at West Newton, was such that the Prince of Wales was appointed a member of the Royal Commission on Housing in 1884, and his sole speech of substance in the House of Lords was on the subject of housing. The school at West Newton built in 1881 is a splendid example of Victoriana. There is also the Dog Handler's cottage and the remains of the only water-mill on the estate, with the wheel and cogs still in position, now a private residence. The club at West Newton was originally the Three Feathers Inn which was purchased by the Prince of Wales in 1883 and substantially modified.

It has set the pattern for the other clubs on the estate. No wines or spirits are allowed to be sold in the clubs and at first there was a rule which said 'one pint of beer per day can be obtained by any one person'. This regulation was easily evaded and King Edward VII substituted one allowing each man to be his own judge of what was good for him, but guarding against intemperance by making a first offence of drunkenness punishable by suspension for one month, a second by suspension for six months, and a third by expulsion.[6]

The Church of St Peter and St Paul was restored in 1881 at the expense of King Edward VII when Prince of Wales. The north aisle, formerly in a 'melancholy and almost hopeless state of dilapidation' was rebuilt under the direction of Sir Arthur Blomfield. A new roof and floor were also provided. The number of monuments installed by the Royal Family is second only to those in Sandringham Church. In 1882 Queen Victoria gave the organ; in 1908 it was overhauled at the expense of King Edward VII, the organ-case being in memory of Canon Hervey, the local Rector for twenty-nine years (1878-1907). The jewelled altar cross was given by the Princess Royal and her husband, Emperor Frederick III of Germany, who courageously reigned for ninety-nine days only, knowing his death from throat cancer was inevitable (1888). The window in the north aisle is a memorial to Colonel Frank R. Beck, M.V.O., the Sandringham Agent, and his men who perished near Gallipoli on 12 August 1915. Dominated by a figure of St George surrounded by sun, moon, and stars, it also depicts Suvla Bay, in the Straits close to where the tragedy occurred. The Royal Household gave the pulpit, and the Bishop of Norwich a Bible and prayer-book. The lych-gate

Jarrolds 1976   Reproduced by gracious permission of
                                     Her Majesty the Queen

Her Majesty the Queen with her horses at Sandringham.

was erected in memory of the dead fallen in the First World War.

Wolferton

Wolferton royal station is in part reopened as a Museum. When Sanger's Circus was departing after the celebrations for the Duke of Clarence's coming-of-age in 1885, an elephant uprooted one of the gold-crowned lamps, and hurled the level-crossing gates into the air.[7]

St Peter's Church, Wolferton, built in carstone, was restored by the Prince of Wales in 1886. The Church's lych-gate of 1896 was made on the estate by local workmen to the design of Sir Arthur Blomfield. The church now contains the oxidized silver eagle, formerly at Sandringham, given by Queen Alexandra in memory of her husband's almost miraculous recovery from typhoid fever in 1871. It is inscribed: 'When I was in trouble I called upon the Lord and he heard me.'

West Newton School

The Dog Handler's Cottage

Bibliography

Alice, Princess (Countess of Athlone): *For my grandchildren*, 1965.
Arthur, Sir George: *Not worth reading*, 1938.
Ashton, Patrick: *St Mary Magdalene, Sandringham Church*, 1968.
Battersea, Lady Constance: *Reminiscences*, 1923.
Battiscombe, Georgina: *Queen Alexandra*, 1969.
Bénézit, Emmanuel: *Dictionnaire critique et documentaire des peintres, sculpteurs, dessinateurs et graveurs*, 3rd ed. 1976.
Blake, P. W., *et al.*: *The Norfolk we live in*, 2nd ed. 1975.
Blomefield, Francis: *The County of Norfolk*, 2nd ed. 1808. (Vol. 9 by Charles Parkin.)
Bloom, Ursula: *The Great Queen Consort*, 1976.
Bolitho, Hector: *The Reign of Queen Victoria*, 1949.
—— (ed.) *The Prince Consort and his brother*, 1933.
Brook-Shepherd, Gordon: *Uncle of Europe*, 1975.
Bryant, A.: *Map of the County of Norfolk*, 1826.
The Builder, 1864, 1867, 1868, 1876, 1891.
Buxton, A.: *The King in his country*, 1955.
Buxton, L. C.: Letter describing ball at Sandringham House dated 3 December 1873, Norfolk Record Office.
Cathcart, Helen: *Sandringham*, 1964.
Cautley, H. Munro: *Norfolk churches*, 1949.
Christopher, Prince of Greece: *Memoirs*, 1938.
Chubb, T., and Stephen, G. A.: *Maps of Norfolk . . . and Norwich plans*, 1928.
Commonwealth War Graves Commission: *Their name liveth*, 1, 1954.
Cooke, C. K.: *Memoir of Princess Mary Adelaide, Duchess of Teck*, 2 vols, 1900.
Cooper, W. E. Shewell: *The Royal gardeners*, 1952.
Corti, E. C.: *The English Empress*, 1945.
Cornwallis-West, Mrs George: *The Reminiscences of Lady Randolph Churchill*, 1973.
Country Life: 'The Gardens at Sandringham, the country home of H.M. King Edward VII' vol. 11 (1902), 806-18.
—— 'The King as a country gentleman', vol. 11 (1902), 714-17.
—— 'The King as a sportsman', vol. 11 (1902), 718-21.
—— 'Sandringham, the country home of H.M. King Edward VII', vol. 11 (1902), 722-35.
——'The Gardens at Sandringham', vol. 75 (1934), 116-24.
Cowles, Virginia: *Edward VII and his circle*, 1956.
Cozens-Hardy, Basil: 'Some Norfolk halls', *Norfolk Archaeology*, vol. 32 (1961), 163-208.
Cresswell, Louisa: *Eighteen years on the Sandringham Estate*, 1887.
—— *Norfolk and the squires, clergy, farmers and labourers . . .* , 1875.
Disraeli, Benjamin (Earl of Beaconsfield): *Letters to Lady Bradford and Lady Chesterfield*, 2 vols., 1929.
Donaldson, Lady Frances: *Edward VIII*, 1974.
Duff, David: *Elizabeth of Glamis*, 1973.
—— *The Shy Princess*, 1974.
—— *Whisper Louise*, 1974.
Duncan, Andrew: *The Reality of the Monarchy*, 1970.
Dutt, W. A.: *The King's Homeland*, 1904.
East Anglian Magazine, 'Hunting in East Anglia', 1 (1936), 39-42.
Edis, R. W.: *Decoration and furniture of town houses*, 1972.
Excursions through Norfolk, vol. 2 (1819).
Fabergé 1846-1920 (Debrett's Peerage Ltd), 1977.
Fisher, Graham and Heather: *Bertie and Alix*, 1974.
—— *The Queen's life*, 1976.
Ford, Colin (ed.): *Happy and glorious; 130 years of royal photographs*, 1977.
Forest, A. J.: *Under three Crowns*, 1961.
Fulford, R. (ed.): *Dearest Child, 1858-61*, 1964.
—— *Dearest Mama, 1861-5*, 1968.
—— *Your Dear Letter, 1865-71*, 1971.
Gernsheim, H. and A.: *Edward VII and Queen Alexandra*, 1962.
—— *Queen Victoria*, 1959.
Girouard, Mark: *The Victorian country house*, 1971.
Gore, J.: *King George V*, 1949.
Grant, Rowland H.: *Church of St Mary Magdalene, Sandringham*, 1936.
Hall, Angus: *The Queen Mother*, 1977.
Handlist to the pictures and works of art at Sandringham, A, 1977.
Hardinge, Lady Helen: *Loyal to three Kings*, 1967.
Hepworth, Philip: 'Story of a Buddha', *Norfolk Fair*, January 1972.

Herbert, Ivor: *The Queen Mother's horses*, 1967.
Hobhouse, Hermione: *Thomas Cubitt master builder*, 1971.
—— 'Notes on Sandringham House, Estate and Church, and on West Newton' (Victorian Society, Summer School, 1976).
Holmes, Sir Richard (ed.): *Edward VII; his life and times*, 2 vols, 1910.
Jarvis, Sir Lewis: Business records, Norfolk Record Office.
Joby, R. S.: *Forgotten Railways: East Anglia*, 1977.
Jones, C. Rachel (Mrs Herbert Jones): *Sandringham past and present*, 2nd ed. 1888.
Jones, I. E.: *A Victorian boyhood*, 3 vols, 1955.
Judd, Denis: *Edward VII, a pictorial biography*, 1975.
Keppel, Sir Henry: *A Sailor's life under four Sovereigns*, 3 vols, 1899.
Lacey, Robert: *Majesty*, 1977.
Ladbrooke, Robert: *Views of the Churches of Norfolk*, 5 vols, 1843.
Laird, Dorothy: *Queen Elizabeth the Queen Mother*, 1966.
Lee, Sir Sidney: *Queen Victoria*, 1904.
Lemere, H.B.: *The Opulent Eye* (text by Nicolas Cooper), 1976.
Lewton-Brain, C. H.: *The Sandringham Estate and its archaeology*, 1954.
Longford, Lady Elizabeth: *The Royal House of Windsor*, 1974.
—— *Victoria, R. I.*, 1964.
Mackie, Charles: *Norfolk annals*, 2 vols, 1901.
McAllister, I.: *Alfred Gilbert*, 1929.
Magnus, Sir Philip: *King Edward the Seventh*, 1964.
Marion, Leslie: 'Round and about Sandringham', *The Temple Magazine*, c. 1896.
Matchett's *Norfolk and Norwich Remembrancer*, 2nd ed. 1822.
Mee, Arthur: *The King's England: Norfolk*, 1972.
Messent, C. J. W.: *A Thousand years of Norfolk carstone*, 1967.
—— *The Architecture on the Royal Estate of Sandringham*, 1974.
Miller, H. Tatlock (ed.): *Royal album*, 1951.
Miller, Philippa: *In search of watermills*, 1972.
Nelson, Horatio (pseud.): *Ode on the Marriage celebration of H.R.H. the Prince of Wales and Princess Alexandra at King's Lynn*, 10 March 1863.
Nicholas II (Emperor of Russia): *Letters to . . . the Empress Marie*, 1937.
Nicolson, Sir Harold: *King George the Fifth*, 1952.
Norwich, Diocese of: *Calendar and clergy list*.
Norwich Mercury: 'Names of the inhabitants of the County of Norfolk who presented the Norwich Gates', 1863.
Ordnance Survey: 'Domesday Book' (facsimile of the part relating to Norfolk) 1862.
—— Six inch and one inch to the mile maps of Sandringham Estate.
Paget, Lady Walburga: *Embassies of other days*, 2 vols, 1923.
—— *The Linings of life*, 2 vols, n.d.
Palmer, Roy: *The Water closet*, 1973.
Palmerston, Lady Emily: *The Letters of Lady Palmerston*, ed. by Tresham Lever, 1957.
Peacock, Lady Irene: *Her Majesty Queen Elizabeth II*, 1952.
—— *The Queen and her children*, 1961.
Pevsner, Sir Nikolaus: *The Buildings of England, North-West and South Norfolk*, 1962.
Ponsonby, Arthur (first Baron Ponsonby): *Henry Ponsonby*, 1942.
Ponsonby, Frederick (first Baron Sysonby): *Recollection of three reigns*, 1951.
Poolman, Kenneth: *Zeppelins over England*, 1960.
Pope-Hennessy, James: *Queen Mary*, 1959.
Procter, Frances and Miller, Philippa: *Village and town signs of Norfolk*, 1973.
Ralph, F.: *Views of Sandringham*, 1905.
Roby, Kinley: *The King, the Press and the People*, 1975.
Roper, Lanning: *Royal gardens*, 1953.
Royal Academy: *This brilliant year; Queen Victoria's jubilee 1887*, 1977.
Royal Archives, Windsor Castle.
Russell, W. H.: 'The Prince of Wales at Sandringham', *Harper's Magazine*, April 1885, 749-73.
Sanderson, Edgar and Melville, Louis: *King Edward VII*, 6 vols, 1911.
Sandringham: Sale plan, 1836, Norfolk Record Office.
—— Title map and award, 1838, Norfolk Record Office.
Sandringham Estate Office: *A Guide to the grounds and a short historical account of Sandringham*, 1967.
Sands, Mollie: 'Royal gardens' in Miller, H. T. (ed.), *Royal album*, 1951.
Saward, H. L.: 'Reminiscences of Wolferton and Sandringham', *G.E.R. Magazine*, vol. 1 (1911), 168-173.
Scase, Tony: 'The Queen: why she loves Sandringham', *East Anglia Monthly*, August 1976.

Shreds and Patches (pseud.): 'Royal travellers on the G.E.R.', *G.E.R. Magazine*, vol. 1 (1911), 174- 81.
Strand Magazine: 'The Prince of Wales at Sandringham', v (1893), 326-39.
Sykes, Christopher: *Four studies in loyalty*, 1946.
Tennyson, Alfred, Lord: *A Welcome to Alexandra*, 1863.
Tigar, Clement: *Henry Walpole 1558-95*, 1970.
Tisdall, E. E. P.: *Queen Victoria's private life*, 1961.
Victoria, Queen: *Letters 1837-61*, III, 1907.
Victoria County History of Norfolk, 2 vols, 1901-6.
Ward, Cyril: *Royal gardens*, 1912.
Ware, Dora: *Short dictionary of British architects*, 1967.
Warren, Mary Spencer: 'Home life at Sandringham', *The Lady's Magazine*, April 1901, 339-45.
Watson, A. E. T.: *King Edward VII as a sportsman*, 1911.
Wentworth Day, James: *King George V as a sportsman*, 1935.

—— *H.R.H. Princess Marina*, 1962.
—— *King's Lynn and Sandringham through the ages*, 1977.
—— 'The Spirit of Sandringham', *East Anglian Magazine*, June 1977, 328-30.
Wheeler, Harold (ed.): *The Life and times of King George V*, 1936.
Wheeler-Bennett, J. W.: *King George VI*, 1958.
White, Francis & Co.: *Directory of Norfolk*, 1864.
Williams, Cicely: *Bishop's wife but still myself*, 1961.
Williamson, Neville: *The Royal residences of Great Britain*, 1960.
Windsor, Edward, Duke of: *A King's Story*, 1951.
Windsor, Wallis, Duchess of: *The Heart has its reasons*, 1956.
Winton, M. J.: *Sandringham House, Norfolk*. 1975.
Woodham-Smith, Cecil: *Queen Victoria; her life and times*, vol. 1 (1819-61), 1972.
Woodward, Kathleen: *Queen Mary*, c. 1923.
The World, 'Sandringham', c. 1875, 10-14.
Young, Arthur: *The Farmer's tour through the East of England*, vol. 2, 1771.

Source Notes

Wensum Books acknowledge with thanks those publishers who have allowed extracts of copyright material to be used.

Foreword
1   Ford, Colin (ed.): *Happy and glorious*, 25-6
Chapter 1. Early History 1752-1862
1   Blomefield, Francis: *The County of Norfolk* 2nd ed. vol. 9, by Charles Parkin, 67
2   Jones, Mrs Herbert: *Sandringham past and present* (1888 ed.) 105-6
3   Cathcart, Helen: *Sandringham*, 48-9
4   ——: *op. cit.*, 105
5   Cathcart: *op. cit.*, 24
6   Young, Arthur: *The Farmer's tour through the East of England* vol. 2, 15
7   Norfolk Record Office: MC 18/29, 18/37
8   Jones: *op. cit.*, 134
9   RA Add: V/132
10 Watson, A. E. T: *King Edward VII as a sportsman*, 17
11 Lever (ed.): *Letters of Lady Palmerston*, 349-50
12 Jones: *op. cit.*, 153
Chapter 2. Royal Search 1861-62
1   RA Add: Q13/ *passim*
2   RA Y 165/29
3   Victoria, Queen: *Letters 1837-61* III, 606
4   Ware, Dora: *Short dictionary of British architects*, 231
5   RA: pp 12458 (16/8; 19/8/62)
6   RA: pp 12458 (28/8/62)
Chapter 3. Building the New House 1863-1870
1   *The Builder* July-December 1891, 343
2   Cresswell, Louisa: *Eighteen years of the Sandringham estate*, 29-30.
3,4 RA Add: pp 1582
5,6 *Norwich Mercury* Names of the inhabitants of the County of Norfolk who presented the Norwich Gates
7   Battiscombe, Georgina: *Queen Alexandra*, 55
8   Cathcart: *op. cit.*, 87
9   RA Add: A3 100
10 RA Add: A3 101
11 Cathcart: *op. cit.*, 85
12 RA Add: C7/75 (12/8/67)
13 Battersea, Constance, Lady: *Reminiscences*, 341, 343
14 Cathcart: *op. cit.*, 91
15 Palmer, Roy: *The Water Closet*, 106
16 Battiscombe: *op. cit.*, 111

Chapter 4. A tour of the new House
1   Lemere, W. Bedford: *Photographs of Sandringham*
2   *Country Life*: 1902, 734
3,6,9 *The World c.* 1875 (offprint)
4   *Country Life*: 1902, 729-30
5   *Fabergé 1846-1920*, 7, 9
7   *Country Life* 1902, 726
8   Ponsonby, Frederick, Lord Sysonby: *Recollections of three reigns*, 134
10 Battiscombe: *op. cit.*, 112
11 Cathcart: *op. cit.*, 94
Chapter 5. A visit to the 'Big House'
1   RA Add: C7/75 (12/8/67)
2   Buxton, Louisa, Caroline: Letter 3.12.1873
3   Disraeli, Benjamin, Earl of Beaconsfield *Letters to Lady Bradford and Lady Chesterfield* 1, 37-8
4   RA Add: J/1463
5   Battersea: *op. cit.*, 356-7
6   Ponsonby: *op. cit.*, 20
7   Brook-Shepherd, Gordon: *Uncle of Europe*, 42-3
8   Cathcart: *op. cit.*, 120-1
9   Magnus, Sir Philip: *King Edward the Seventh* Paperback ed., 123
10 Cresswell: *op. cit.*, 69-70
11 Ibid: 180
12 Watson: *op. cit.*, 24
13 Ibid: 38
Chapter 6. Albert Edward Prince of Wales 1870-1901
1   *The Builder*: 1878
2   Cathcart: *op. cit.*, 118
3   Ibid: 125
4   RA Z 457/29
5   RA A4/36
6   Mackie, Charles: *Norfolk annals* II, 420, 424
7   Magnus: *op. cit.*, 279
8   Pope-Hennessy, James: *Queen Mary*, 356-7
9,10 RA: Geo V CC 6/53
11 Pope-Hennessy: *op. cit.*, 276
12 RA: Z 457/23
13 Watson: *op. cit.*, 143
14 Ford: *op. cit.*, 356-7
Chapter 7. King Edward VII 1901-10
1   Cowles, Virginia: *Edward VII and his circle*, 336
2   RA: pp Ed. VII c 19226
3   RA Z 457/30
4,5 RA Z 457/46
6   RA Add. L/2/53

7   RA Add. A/15/8341
8   Dutt, W. A.: *The King's homeland*, 183-4
9   Watson: *op. cit.*, 224-5
10 *Sandringham* (guide 1978), (16)
11 Nicolson, Sir Harold: *King George the fifth*, 105
Chapter 8. King George V 1910-36
1   *Sandringham* (guide 1978), (inside cover)
2   Nicolson: *op. cit.*, 51
3   Poolman, Kenneth: *Zeppelins over England*, 41
4   RA: Geo. V CC 50/1158
5   Wentworth Day, James: *King George V as a sports-man*, 28
6   RA: Geo. V N2556/49
7   Battiscombe: *op. cit.*, 124
8   Wentworth Day: *op. cit.*, 267
9   RA: Add. A/21/228
10 RA: Geo. V CC 6/53
11 RA: Geo. V CC 50/1527
12 Pope-Hennessy: *op. cit.*, 541
Chapter 9. King Edward VIII 1936
1   Donaldson, Frances, Lady: *Edward VIII* paperback ed. 292
Chapter 10. King George VI 1936-52
1   Cathcart: *op. cit.*, 203
2   Buxton, A: *The King in his country*, 4
3   Roper, Lanning: *Royal gardens*, 7
Chapter 13. The Royal Parishes
1   Tigar, Clement: *Henry Walpole*, 10-15
2   Cozens-Hardy, Basil: *Some Norfolk halls*, 163-208
3   Norfolk Record Office MC 18/12
4   RA: Z 475/246-61
5   Cresswell *op. cit.*, 144
6   Dutt: *op. cit.*, 130
7   Shreds and patches, (pseud): 'Royal Visitors to Wolferton' *Great Eastern Railway Magazine* vol.1.

Index

Items beginning with the word Sandringham and British monarchs and their consorts from Queen Victoria are excluded. Illustrations are designated by BOLD type.